DISPLACED PERSONS

DISPLACED PERSONS:

THE LIBERATION AND ABUSE OF HOLOCAUST SURVIVORS

TED GOTTFRIED

ILLUSTRATIONS BY STEPHEN ALCORN

THE HOLOCAUST
Twenty-First Century Books
Brookfield, Connecticut

Title page and chapter opening illustrations by Stephen Alcorn © www.alcorngallery.com

Photographs courtesy of Harry S. Truman Library: pp. 16, 39;
USHMM: pp. 29, 51 (© American Jewish Joint Distribution
Committee), 63, 79; Hulton Getty/Archive Photos: pp. 86, 100

Library of Congress Cataloging-in-Publication Data
Gottfried, Ted.
Displaced persons : the liberation and abuse of Holocaust survivors / Ted Gottfried.
p. cm.
Includes bibliographical references (p.) and index.
ISBN 0-7613-1924-7 (lib. bdg.)
1. Refugees, Jewish—Europe—History—20th century—Juvenile literature. 2. Holocaust survivors—
Europe—Juvenile literature. 3. Jews—Europe—Migrations—Juvenile literature. 4. World War, 1939-
1945—Refugees—Europe—Juvenile literature. 5. Palestine—Emigration and immigration—Juvenile
literature. [1. Refugees, Jewish. 2. Holocaust survivors. 3. Jews—Migrations. 4. World War, 1939-1945—
Refugees. 5. Palestine—Emigration and immigration.] I. Title.
DS135.E83 .G66 2001   940'.04924—dc21   00-051225

Published by Twenty-First Century Books
A Division of The Millbrook Press, Inc.
2 Old New Milford Road
Brookfield, Connecticut 06804
www.millbrookpress.com

For my dear friend Denise Nolan,
who raised the questions
which led to the writing of this book

ACKNOWLEDGMENTS

I am grateful to personnel of the Judaica Room of the New York Central Research Library, the Mid-Manhattan Library, the Jewish Museum, and the Society Library in New York, and the United States Holocaust Memorial Museum in Washington, D.C., for their aid in gathering material for this book. Thanks are also due—with much love—to my wife, Harriet Gottfried, who—as always—read and critiqued this book. Her help was invaluable, but any shortcomings in the work are mine alone.

—Ted Gottfried

CONTENTS

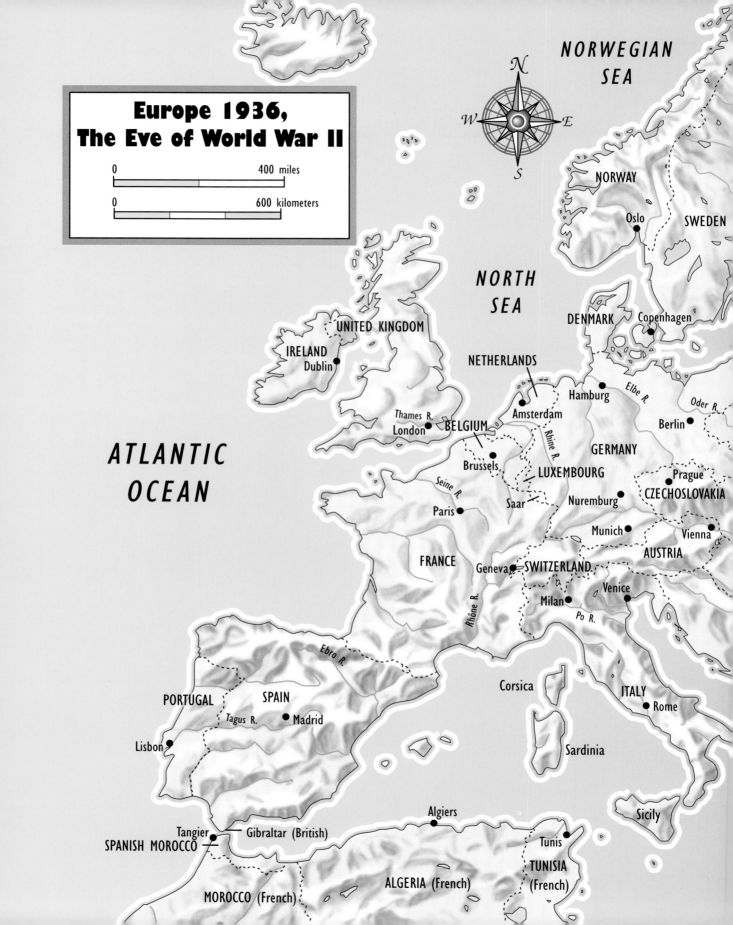

Europe 1936,
The Eve of World War II

0   400 miles

0   600 kilometers

NORWEGIAN SEA

N
W   E
S

NORWAY

Oslo

SWEDEN

NORTH SEA

DENMARK   Copenhagen

UNITED KINGDOM

IRELAND
Dublin

NETHERLANDS

Hamburg   Elbe R.

Oder R.

Amsterdam

Berlin

Thames R.
London   BELGIUM

GERMANY

Rhine R.

Brussels   LUXEMBOURG

Prague

Seine R.   Saar   Nuremburg   CZECHOSLOVAKIA

Paris

Munich   Vienna

ATLANTIC OCEAN

FRANCE

Geneva   SWITZERLAND   AUSTRIA

Venice

Milan   Po R.

Rhône R.

Ebro R.

Corsica   ITALY

PORTUGAL   SPAIN

Rome

Tagus R.   Madrid

Lisbon

Sardinia

Algiers

Sicily

Tangier   Gibraltar (British)
SPANISH MOROCCO

Tunis

TUNISIA (French)

MOROCCO (French)   ALGERIA (French)

THE END OF THE WAR

1

. . . The Russians entered, and we were in such a condition that no one moved, no one went out. We did not laugh, we were apathetic—and the Russians came. A general came in, he was Jewish. He told us that he was delighted, as this was the first camp in which he had found people still alive. He started to cry; but we didn't. He wept and we didn't.[1]

—Bela Braver describes the reaction of her fellow
concentration camp inmates on the day of liberation.

**W**orld War II lasted nearly six years in Europe. It began in September 1939 and ended in May 1945. It was won by the Allied armies of Russia, Great Britain, France, and the United States. It was lost by Nazi Germany, Fascist Italy, and various satellite countries who fought alongside the Nazis.

By the end of 1944, the war was winding down. The German army was being decimated by lack of supplies, starvation, and exposure throughout the cruel winter. By spring it was in full retreat from the advancing Russian armies. With the addition of fresh U.S. troops, the Allied forces had overcome the German counterattack known as the Battle of the Bulge, driven the Germans from France and Belgium, and were now penetrating deep into Germany. Naval blockades and Allied military actions had cut supply lines to the German civilian population as well.

As the war drew to a close in Europe, panic swept over the continent. In Western Europe the population scrambled to get out of the way of the retreating German army. In Germany itself the carpet bombing of cities by American and British planes was creating some two million homeless German refugees. In Eastern Europe the situation was even worse. Eleven million Russian soldiers and seven million Russian civilians had been killed by the German army during the invasion of Russia. Now civilians in Hungary, Romania, Bulgaria, Austria, and other countries allied with the Germans were fleeing a Russian army bent on vengeance as it advanced toward the German border and Berlin.

The Liberation of Majdanek

As early as July 1944, the Russian army had been pushing the German invaders back through Poland. On July 24 the Russians reached the Nazi death camp of Majdanek in eastern Poland. This was the first such camp to be liberated by Allied forces.

The camp had been built in 1941 to hold five thousand Russian soldiers taken prisoner by the Nazis. The prisoners were brutally treated. Some died from the vicious beatings they received. Most died of hunger and typhus. All five thousand perished within months of their imprisonment.

In February 1942, Majdanek became a major extermination camp. From then on its inmates were Jews. Between then and July 24, 1944, a half million Jewish men, women, and children were shot to death or killed in the gas chambers there. On the day of liberation the Russian troops found fewer than six hundred Jews still alive.

Five and a half years earlier, on January 30, 1939, German Führer Adolf Hitler, addressing the Reichstag (German parliament), promised that the war, which was soon to begin, would accomplish "the destruction of the Jewish race in Europe."[2] By the end of the war the Nazis had translated those words into the Holocaust. Two-thirds of the prewar population of European Jews had been slaughtered by German soldiers and their accomplices. In all, more than six million Jews had died at the hands of the Nazis.

Methods of Murder

Some Jews died in the ghettos created by the Nazis in such cities as Warsaw and Lublin in Poland. Some were killed in massacres by firing squads like the one at Babi Yar in the Ukraine. There, over a period of two days, machine-gun squads of Germans and their Ukrainian helpers mowed down 34,000 Jewish men, women, and children. Similar squads operated on a smaller scale in Poland, but were replaced by gas vans, which could hold 80 to 150 Jews at a time while they were slowly killed with carbon monoxide.

During the last winter of the war, as the German army fled the Russians, there was a forced march from Eastern Europe to the West by thousands of sick, ill-clothed, half-starved Jewish prisoners. It was bitter cold and many of the prisoners froze to death. Stragglers were shot or left by the side of the road to die. This was only one example of how the Nazis' determination to annihilate the Jews took precedence over the waging of the war. Just as unyielding was the policy of holding up shipments of supplies—including ammunition, food, and medicine—for the outnumbered German army fighting desperately against the Russians in the East while trains of boxcars loaded with Jews destined for the gas chambers tied up the rail lines.

When American soldiers liberated the Dachau concentration camp in April 1945, they found fifty unloaded boxcars, which had been left on a siding by the German guards when they fled. They had been standing there for several days. It was reported that "there were about one hundred people in each boxcar and of the five thousand prisoners, about three thousand were already dead upon the arrival of the army." Half of those still alive died within the next few days.[3]

Written in the Totenbuch

Dachau was only one of the German-run concentration camps in which the majority of the six million slaughtered Jews were killed. There were hundreds of these camps in Germany, Austria, and Poland. Most of them were small work camps and transit camps. Only thirty were major death camps like Dachau in which prisoners were either worked to death, starved to death, or murdered in cold blood. All thirty kept a record, called a *Totenbuch* (death book) of those

Starved prisoners liberated from the Ebensee concentration camp in the Austrian Alps

killed. Six of them, all in Poland, were major extermination camps with gas chambers and ovens to dispose of the victims' bodies. In all thirty of these camps, the overwhelming majority of victims were Jews.

Death was a presence felt by the liberators of all of the camps. Bergen-Belsen survivor Anita Lasker-Wallfisch quotes from *Notes on Belsen,* an official report on what the British 63d Anti-Tank Regiment found when they liberated the camp: "There were appr. 50,000 people in the camp of which about 10,000 lay dead in the huts or about the camp. Those still alive had no food or water for about seven days, after a long period of semi-starvation. Typhus, among other diseases, was raging . . . filth everywhere . . . the air was poisoned. . . ."[4]

At Buchenwald, where 50,000 people were murdered, American troops found that "slave laborers, laying on their barracks bunks, could barely raise their heads to see their liberators. Their muscle was eaten away. Maggots settled in the corners of their sunken eyes as they watched the G.I.s tread silently by them."[5]

Starving, Eating, Dying

In the aftermath of liberation, thousands who had survived the Nazi death camps perished. They were too far gone with typhus and tuberculosis to be saved. They were starving skeletons, their tight-stretched skin eaten away by lice. The rescuers constantly faced the question of whether to feed them first or delouse them first.

Ephraim Poremba, an inmate at the Allach camp when it was liberated by the U.S. army, described what happened when the survivors were fed: "The Americans today gave out food such as you had never eaten in your whole life. What was it? It was pork fat with noodles. From the pork fat with noodles people began to get sick, there was already typhus, and people began to get diarrhea, a lot of people got diarrhea, our stomachs weren't ready for fat. People began to die in large numbers."[6]

Haya Koplowitz, liberated at Bergen-Belsen by the British army in April 1945, remembered how the first act of the starving prisoners who had been freed was to find food: "Whoever had a little strength started to look for food in the kitchens. They opened kitchens, went into the storerooms where cabbage was kept. They ate and they ate, and from that they died."[7]

Their systems were not able to digest the food, but they were starving and could not stop eating. Their stomachs ruptured, killing them. They were among the more than 13,000 inmates who perished at Bergen-Belsen within days of liberation.

"Free, and Yet Not Free"

For the American and British liberators, the immediate problem was what to do with the survivors of the concentration camps. Many suffered from a variety of diseases, and if they were allowed to simply leave the camps, there was the possibility of contaminating the general population. There was fear of starting an epidemic. There was also fear that once free of jurisdiction former inmates might embark on revenge killings. The Allied authorities decided to keep the survivors where they were. In this way, the death camps became displaced persons (DP) facilities.

The DPs were baffled by this decision. Ephraim Poremba described the effect it had: "Apparently they [the Americans] consulted among themselves and decided not to let us disperse. . . . Immediately they formed a chain around the outside of the camp and told us to get back inside. . . . Why are they making us go back inside the camp? Why don't they let us go wherever we want? But where to go? After all, the war is not yet over. We can still hear shooting. . . . [The Americans] are here and we are free and yet not free. The Americans are already stationed around the camp."[8]

It was a temporary solution. During the last days of the war, it was perhaps a necessary one. But long after the war was over, there were places where this "temporary" solution was still in effect.

Victors, Vanquished, and Victims

Confinement by their rescuers may have been the last straw for some of the survivors. Considering the ordeal they had been through, it's not surprising that mental illness was widespread among them. Signs of deep-seated depression and apathy were to be seen everywhere in the camps. These people had survived, but they had lost their loved ones—they had lost everything—and the memory of the horrors they had been through left them to ask themselves if life was really worth living. Many committed suicide.

Others had trouble dealing with the reality of their situation. In some cases it was particularly hard to accept the relationship between their liberators and the Germans who surrendered to them. Years later Buchenwald survivor Max Nabig—a Dutchman who had undergone experimental operations without anesthetic by Nazi doctors trying to determine the pain threshold under such conditions—spoke bitterly about how considerately American officers dealt with the Germans. He remembered how they seemed to "regard the whole war effort as a sports competition in which the winners, in a show of civilized chivalry, were to shake hands with the losers."[9] That the torturers and murderers he had known should be regarded like gallant competitors in a football or soccer game filled Max Nabig with rage.

In fairness, this was not usually the case. Americans liberating Dachau were greeted by a German officer surrendering according to formal military protocol. He appeared in full uniform, complete with medals and ribbons, looking for all the world as if he was about to lead a parade. He gave the Nazi salute along with a heartfelt "Heil Hitler." The American officer to whom he was surrendering "looked down and around at mounds of rotting corpses, at thousands of prisoners shrouded in their own filth. He hesitated only a moment, then spat in the Nazi's face, snapping *'Schweinehund'* (pig-dog) before ordering him taken away."[10]

There was no single Allied or American response to the death camps by the soldiers who liberated them. As the war wound down, there was no single policy yet in place for dealing with the enemy, or with the survivors. The enormity of the Jewish DP problem would only begin to be appreciated after May 8, 1945, when the war in Europe officially ended.

2

DP
CAMPS

It is better to be a conquered German than a liberated Jew.[1]

—Held behind barbed wire by his liberators,
a Jewish DP defines his situation.

At the end of the war, Europe was in chaos. The continent was "a churning maelstrom of eight million displaced persons" of various nationalities.[2] The majority of these refugees fled to those areas of Austria and Germany that had come under the control of the British and Americans, rather than the Russians. This was because the Russians, in response to brutal Nazi policies, which had cost the lives of 11 million soldiers and 7 million Soviet civilians, were equally brutal in their treatment of enemy civilians as their victorious forces marched westward through countries that had been allied with Germany. Included in the 8 million recognized as DPs by the non-Russian Allies were prisoners of war captured by the Germans; civilians transported to Germany to be used as forced labor by the Nazis; Eastern Europeans who had voluntarily worked in German industry; citizens of other countries who had collaborated with the Germans and were now afraid to return to their homes; Germans, Austrians, Hungarians, Romanians, and others who had fled the Russian army; Germans and Austrians whose living quarters had been taken over by the Russian army; and Germans whose homes had been destroyed by Allied bombings.

Among these refugees were approximately 100,000 Jewish survivors of the Nazi death camps. As the months passed, their numbers would multiply. Jews who had managed to hide throughout the war, Jews who had fought with anti-Nazi groups, Eastern European Jews who had seen neighbors collaborate with the Nazis to take over their property and so had good reason to know that they would not be welcomed back, Russian Jews fleeing religious persecution by the Communist government would all add to the number of Jewish refugees. Along with the non-Jewish DPs, they would seek refuge in the American and British occupation zones in the aftermath of the war. The Jewish DPs, however, were small in number compared to the German refugees. Indeed, the original number of Jewish DPs was negligible considering the millions of European DPs that had converged on the non-Russian Allied occupation zones.

What made the Jews different from other displaced persons was that as a group they had no real homeland in Europe. The variety of places in which they had settled over the centuries had rarely accepted them as equals. Their history in these places—right up to the outbreak of World War II—had been one of persecution and second-class citizenship. Hostility greeted many who tried to return to the villages and cities where they had lived before the war. Many Jews were afraid to return. Many did not want to go back to such places and such lives. As a practical matter, at this moment in time, they had no place to go, no homeland. But that would change.

A Doctor's Dilemma

By the summer of 1945, the major cities of Germany had been bombed into rubble. Commanding General of the Allied Forces Dwight D. Eisenhower estimated a "loss of housing in bombed-out cities averaging well over 50 percent."[3] The German and Austrian people were scavenging for food and clothing. They were dependent on the occupying Allied forces for medicine and medical treatment.

In Vienna, the capital of Austria, the once prestigious Rothschild Hospital was requisitioned to house refugees and to provide medical treatment for them. Dr. Otto Wolken, a German-Jewish physician who had survived the Auschwitz death camp, worked at the Rothschild Hospital after the war ended. He described conditions there. "I have X-rayed 2,000 people at random here," he testified. "Of them 1,400 have tuberculosis now, or are arrested cases. The sanitary conditions are incredible. We have 15 toilets for 4,000 people. Half of these people are suffering from malnutrition. You can imagine their mental state. . . ."[4]

The Jewish DP Predicament

Conditions in the DP camps were even worse. There were shortages of food as well as medicine. Camp infirmaries were overburdened and short of qualified medical personnel. Many of these holding facilities were former concentration camps. The first groups of DPs held there were Jewish survivors of the Holocaust.

As the camps filled up with other refugees, however, the Jews became more and more of a minority. At first, due to a lack of preplanning and of adequately trained personnel, refugees of a variety of nationalities were thrown together in the DP complexes. Nazis, collaborators, and other anti-Semites (Jew haters) were not weeded out from among these newcomers. The Jews were forced to share quarters with them. Sometimes the Jews were still wearing their "concentration camp garb—a rather hideous striped pajama effect," and sometimes they were "obliged to wear German S. S. uniforms," according to a report on the camps. (SS uniforms had been worn by military units assigned to exterminate Jews.) The report went on to observe that "it is questionable which clothing they hate more."[5] These clothes identified them to the other prisoners as Jewish survivors.

The language differences among those billeted together often resulted in fights. The authorities decided to separate them and assign them barracks according to nationality. General Eisenhower issued orders that Jews be categorized according to the country from which they had originated—often the country from which they had fled. The general felt that identifying them separately as Jews would lend credence to Hitler's anti-Semitic racial theories. Thus

Jews found themselves once again a minority among Poles, Hungarians, Ukrainians, and even Austrians or Germans. Easily identifiable by what they wore, and by their starved and skeletal condition, they often found themselves once again confronted by anti-Semitism.

A German Infrastructure

Monitoring anti-Semitism in the DP camps was not a priority for the Allied army personnel charged with administering them. Obtaining food, medicine, and other supplies took precedence. This meant dealing with German and Austrian suppliers. Even if the goods came from other European countries, they had to be bought through German and Austrian middlemen—shippers, wholesalers, and retailers.

The problem was that not many of those in charge spoke German. The armies were short of interpreters. The solution was to use Germans and Austrians who spoke English. In the disastrous postwar German economy it was easy to find educated Germans who were up to the task. The military, short of trained personnel, also used Germans to help run the DP camps. However, there wasn't enough time to run efficient background checks on those Germans who were employed in a variety of positions, which gave them varying degrees of power over the DPs. The more experienced they were, the more likely they were to have been involved in jobs related to Nazi administration of the camps.

Inevitably, former Nazis managed to land jobs in the DP facilities. The degree to which they persecuted Jews varied, but it was frequent enough to cause protests in many of the camps. Some acted for the Allies in purchasing goods and services from former Nazis. Others favored non-Jews over Jews when they distributed clothing and food. Jewish children, many of them orphans who had lost their parents to the gas chambers, were hassled and sometimes physically assaulted by non-Jewish children in the camps, and by adults as well. For the most part, Germans placed in positions of authority by the Allied military did not interfere with the harassment of Jewish DPs.

The Jewish Agencies

Jewish DPs, including the children, lived with the torment of not knowing whether their closest relatives—mothers, fathers, sisters, brothers, sons, daughters, and others—were alive or dead. In the first weeks following liberation they had no way of sending or receiving mail. They were still being held behind barbed wire, forbidden to leave the camps lest they spread disease or commit revenge killings. They were still being mixed in with the general DP camp population, indistinguishable from the other refugees flooding into the camps. Their unique situation and special needs as Jewish Holocaust survivors were either unrecognized or ignored by the Allied authorities.

Their plight was not, however, unrecognized by other Jews. According to camp records, "a considerable number and variety of Jewish agencies were active among the DPs. First to reach the Jewish survivors were the Jewish military chaplains, and it was they who established the first link between the survivors and the outside world. In June 1945 a delegation of the Jewish Brigade Group [Jewish soldiers from Palestine who had fought with the British against the Nazis] arrived in the DP camps—the first group of Palestinian Jews to establish contact with the survivors. The American Jewish Joint Distribution Committee (known as The Joint), headed by its European director, Joseph J. Schwartz, sent its first teams to the camps in June 1945. By August 1945 its operations gained official recognition and were expanded. In the British zone, a Jewish Relief Unit sponsored by British Jewry was engaged in welfare operations."[6]

The Jewish groups coordinated their activities with the United Nations Relief and Rehabilitation Agency (UNRRA), which had been organized in 1943 by the forty-four Allied nations fighting against the Nazis. Even then, two years before the United Nations itself came into existence, concerned civilians had anticipated that the end of the war would produce a tremendous refugee problem. UNRRA established a Central Tracing Bureau to help DPs find relatives in Germany, Austria, and Italy. The bureau received over 50,000 search requests in its first four months. It was later incorporated into the International Tracing Service (ITS), a permanent organization that operated worldwide.

"Everyone Cried . . ."

The various organizations brought pressure to improve conditions in the DP compounds. Restrictions on sending and receiving mail began to be relaxed. Inmates who were not ill were allowed to come and go at many of the camps. Illinois State University Professor of History Mark Wyman describes in his study of DPs how "large numbers of refugees tramped from camp to camp, searching for kin or others from their past."[7]

One searcher was Kopel Kandelcukier, who left the Theresienstadt camp in Czechoslovakia with a few other Jewish survivors from the town of Bialobrzegi in Poland. "We went back to Poland just in case there were any survivors from our families," the teenager testified. "The Poles were very hostile to us, and I was glad to get back to the safety of Theresienstadt [where] there were a large number of boys and girls without parents, with nowhere to go."[8]

Some Holocaust survivors were more fortunate. They succeeded in making contact with other family members who had escaped death. Eva Goldberg, who survived Auschwitz, was one of them: "People came from the Red Cross and called out names, maybe someone was still alive. Of course I gave them the name of my brother, because father had surely not [survived]. A month later they called my name over the loudspeaker. . . . I went to the office and they handed me a telegram. It was from my brother! The Red Cross had found my brother at Cluj! I left the office holding the cable like a flag, and shouting: 'I'm not alone anymore, I have a brother, I'm not alone anymore.' Everyone cried. . . ."[9]

Rehabilitating the Germans

Although conditions in the camps improved, progress seemed slow to the Jewish DPs. Prisoners of war from the Allied countries who had been held by the

A worker for The Joint gives food to a three-year-old Jewish DP child in Vienna.

Germans were being quickly sent home. Many of them were Russian, and because of Communist repression not all of them wanted to return to their homeland. They were sent back anyway. Poles whom the Nazis had transported to Germany as slave laborers were also quickly transported back to Poland. Before long, mostly homeless Germans and Austrians and occasional Nazi collaborators remained in the DP camps with the Jews. Even their population was constantly changing, however, and in the meantime the Jewish DP numbers were growing with new arrivals from Eastern Europe. These Eastern European Jews soon made up a large majority of the DP population.

Both the original Jewish DPs and the new arrivals could not help being aware of the beginnings of a massive Allied effort to rehabilitate Germany. Tensions with Communist Russia were straining the World War II alliance. Russia occupied most of Eastern Europe after the war, Germany was split in two, and East Germany was being transformed into a Communist state. West Germany was regarded by the other Allied powers as a necessary bulwark against any further spread of Russian Communist domination. As a result, the West German economy would be refinanced. West German industry would be rebuilt. The West German people would be fed, and housed as quickly as buildings could be erected from the rubble. Jobs would be created to help restore West Germany to prosperity.

Less than three months after the armistice was signed ending the war in Europe, some four million German refugees had already been repatriated. From their barbed-wire compounds Jewish DPs dressed in ragtag clothing observed a population of Germans who appeared increasingly well fed and well dressed. This had been the enemy who killed six million Jews—men, women, and children. Now they seemed to be bouncing back from defeat while many of the Jewish DPs slept on the same bunks they had as concentration camp prisoners, and subsisted on a diet of 2,000 calories per day of which 1,250 consisted of "a black, wet and extremely unappetizing bread."[10]

The military—American and British—disregarded their plight. Those in charge felt that they must "live with the Germans while the DPs (displaced persons) are a more temporary problem."[11] Nevertheless, much attention was being focused on the DP crisis by the media. President Harry S. Truman took notice. In the summer of 1945, he sent Earl G. Harrison, dean of the University of Pennsylvania Law School, as his personal envoy to the Intergovernmental Committee on Refugees inquiring into the conditions of the Jews in the DP camps in the American zone in Germany. The report submitted by Harrison to Truman—the Harrison Report, as it came to be known—changed the way the Jewish DPs were treated and had a major effect on their future.

THE HARRISON REPORT

3

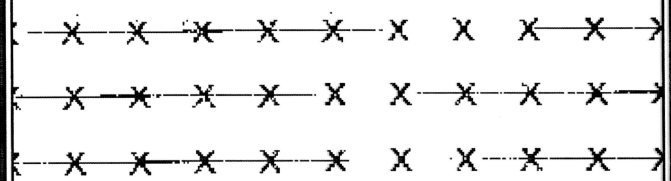

As matters now stand, we appear to be treating the Jews as the Nazis treated them, except that we do not exterminate them. They are in concentration camps, in large numbers under our military guard instead of SS troops. One is led to wonder whether the German people, seeing this, are not supposing that we are following or at least condoning Nazi policy."[1]

—Earl G. Harrison to President Harry S. Truman

Earl G. Harrison's successful career as a private attorney had led to his appointment as dean of the University of Pennsylvania Law School. In 1940–1941, he had served as director of alien registration in the U.S. Department of Justice. He became special assistant to the attorney general and was then appointed commissioner of the Immigration and Naturalization Service, serving from 1942 to 1944. In that job he had established a reputation for fair-mindedness, which earned him the respect of many of those high up in the Truman administration.

As President Truman's special envoy, Harrison's assignment was "to inquire into needs of the non-repatriables with particular reference to the stateless and Jewish refugees."[2] He was accompanied on this mission by Dr. Joseph Schwartz of the American Jewish Joint Distribution Committee. The Joint had been formed by a variety of religious, political, and other lay organizations to provide help for the widely persecuted and battle-ravaged European Jewish civilian population during World War I. It ranked second in size only to the Red Cross as a world relief organization. Following World War II, The Joint focused its efforts on the survivors of the Holocaust.

Food and Shelter

With Dr. Schwartz as a guide, Harrison made a three-week inspection tour of the DP camps. In August 1945 he completed his report. It confirmed that three months after the end of the war Jewish DPs were being "treated virtually as war prisoners, subjected to intimidation by non-Jewish DPs and to the confinement, uniforms, and food ration of prisoners."[3]

The Harrison Report is the account of a man shocked by what he had seen and who was determined not to tone it down. At the same time, Earl Harrison was a practical man used to dealing with the reality of situations. "It is difficult to evaluate the food situation fairly," he reported, "because one must be mindful of the fact that quite generally food is scarce and is likely to be more so during the winter ahead. On the other hand, in presenting the factual situation, one must raise the question as to how much longer many of these people, particularly those who have over such a long period felt persecution and near starvation, can survive on a diet composed principally of bread and coffee."[4]

The approach of winter also raised Harrison's concerns about adequate shelter. He found much of the DP housing "clearly unfit for winter use," and reported "great concern about the prospect of a complete lack of fuel." He pointed out that "close to a million displaced persons will be in Germany and Austria when winter sets in."[5]

Unsympathetic Subordinates

The Harrison Report was to prove a strong influence on President Truman. It would banish forever the last traces of the anti-Semitism that had been part of his upbringing in southern Missouri. This change in attitude was demonstrated publicly as early as April 1943 when then-Senator Truman spoke at a huge rally in Chicago "to urge help for the doomed Jews of Europe." In his speech, there was "an implied criticism of the President [Franklin D. Roosevelt] for doing too little to help the Jews."[6] Now president himself, Truman would act on the Harrison Report in a variety of ways that would stir up controversy.

On August 31, 1945, President Truman wrote to General Eisenhower, the man who seven years later would succeed him as president. Truman pointed out that some of the conditions described in the Harrison Report were not in accordance with military policies because "the policies are not being carried out by some of your subordinate officers." He reminded the general that his officers had been "directed to requisition billeting facilities from the German population for the benefit of displaced persons." He pointed out that quarters had not been obtained from the Germans for DPs, and quoted the Harrison Report as to the horrendous conditions in the facilities where the DPs were forced to live. The president directed Eisenhower "to get these people out of camps and into decent houses . . . These houses," he insisted, "should be requisitioned from the German civilian population."[7]

One of those not carrying out official policy was Colonel Epes, the officer in charge of the DP camps at Hart and Haag in Austria. He had little patience with Jews who refused to go back to the countries from which they had fled. On October 3, 1945, he ordered that the Jewish inmates of the facilities under his command be transferred to Camp 55. The local director of The Joint protested that Camp 55 was unlivable, a compound made up of "barbed wire, pill boxes, leaky roofs, [and] broken windows." When the UNRRA representative backed him up, Epes responded that "his men would be armed with live ammunition to enforce the order."[8]

The Jews stood up to his threat. They staged a sit-down strike to keep from being moved to Camp 55. Press coverage of their action brought it to the attention of General Mark Clark, who was in charge of the American zone in Austria. The general publicly reprimanded Colonel Epes. "I don't give a god-damn whether or not you are interested in or in sympathy with my orders on Jews," he told him. "You will obey them." Soon after, Epes took over hotels in the resort town of Bad Gasten to provide rooms for the Jewish DPs.[9]

"Old Blood and Guts"

Not all American generals were as faithful to military policy toward Jews and Germans as Mark Clark was. One of these was General George "Old Blood and Guts" Patton. Ruthless and inflexible, Patton had made headlines during the war while inspecting a military hospital. When he was told that one of the patients was suffering from shell shock, Patton accused the young soldier of cowardice and struck him in the face. Although reprimanded, Patton was a brilliant tactician and was subsequently given command of the Third Army in Europe. While in that position, Patton had publicly questioned whether African Americans were fit to serve in the military. After the war ended, he wrote to his wife that "the Germans are the only decent people left in Europe. It's a choice between them and the Russians. I prefer the Germans."[10]

General Patton voiced "outspoken opposition to the official policy of denazification"—the program designed to replace anti-Semitic and racist Nazi theories and institutions with democratic ideals and government in Germany.[11] Patton had been assigned as military governor of Bavaria, a job which put him in charge of DP camps in that German state. He saw to it that they were ruled with an iron hand, and many of the horrendous conditions described in the Harrison Report were at their worst in the facilities under Patton.

When Eisenhower responded to the Harrison Report by ordering his subordinates, including Patton, to make certain reforms, Patton was loath to comply. In his diary he wrote that "Harrison and his ilk believe that the DP is a human being, which he is not, and this applies particularly to the Jews, who are lower than animals."[12] When he continued not implementing official policy, Patton was relieved of responsibility. Soon after, on December 21, 1945, he died as the result of injuries sustained in an automobile accident.

Eisenhower Responds

On October 8, 1945, General Eisenhower responded to President Truman's letter with a "full report on matters pertaining to the care and welfare of the Jewish victims of Nazi persecution within the United States zone of Germany." He argued that "the housing problem must be seen in full perspective." By winter, he predicted, "one million and a half German air-raid refugees" and 600,000 ethnic Germans fleeing Poland, Czechoslovakia, and Yugoslavia would have

As United States General Dwight D. Eisenhower (center) looks on, survivors of a concentration camp in Gotha, Germany, demonstrate how they were tortured by Nazis. General George S. Patton stands to the far left.

flocked to the American zone. These were in addition to "152,000 more Germans from Austria." According to the general, the Jewish DPs were allotted more floor space in the holding facilities than American soldiers in their barracks. He also cited the need to keep the DPs in a central location so that food, medicine, and various services might be delivered to them more efficiently than if the DPs were scattered among requisitioned housing.[13]

The policy, still in effect at that time in many places, of restricting DPs from leaving the camps was defended by Eisenhower. "One reason for limiting the numbers permitted to leave our assembly centers," he wrote the president, "was depredation and banditry by displaced persons themselves." He claimed that more than two thousand DPs had died from (presumed stolen) "poisonous liquor." Eisenhower added that "many others died by violence or were injured while circulating outside our assembly centers."[14]

Eisenhower went on to claim that there had been many reforms since Harrison's inspection tour. He had raised the daily food allowance from 2,000 to 2,500 calories per day. Clothing and shoes were now being made available to Jewish DPs. They were receiving "excellent medical attention."[15]

From the tone of Eisenhower's letter, it seemed as if the Harrison Report had put him on the defensive. In a subsequent communication he appeared to be more sympathetic. He spoke of how he had seen "thousands of men and women who had suffered in the German concentration camps," adding that he did not know "when the stateless Jews will be given a permanent home," but that until that time he was determined "to make it possible for them to lead a normal and useful life." It was a sincere pledge, but one which would meet many obstacles in the day-to-day life of the DP camps.[16]

One of Eisenhower's measures that did take effect quickly owed much of its success to supervision by The Joint. Eisenhower had ordered the separating of Jewish DPs from the rest of the DP population. Special centers were established for "those Jews who are without nationality or those not Soviet citizens who do not desire to return to their country of origin."[17]

Eleanor Roosevelt vs. the Russians

The question of what to do with Jews who were Russian citizens was still on hold five months after Harrison submitted his report. That was when President Truman appointed Eleanor Roosevelt as a delegate to the first meeting of the United Nations (UN) General Assembly in London. Mrs. Roosevelt was the wife of the late president, Franklin D. Roosevelt, and a distinguished writer, lecturer, and social activist in her own right.

Soon after reaching London, Mrs. Roosevelt was assigned to Committee Three of the UN Assembly. This was the committee dealing with humanitarian concerns. It was one of the first postwar political battlegrounds between the United States and Communist Russia. Mrs. Roosevelt soon found herself doing battle with the Russian representative, Andrei Vishinsky.

The issue was what to do with the millions of European DPs, including the Jews. In the Russian view there were only two kinds of refugees—those eager to go back to the countries they had come from, and "traitors, war criminals, or collaborators."[18] But of course there was a third group—those who were both anti-Nazi and anti-Communist and who faced violence and death if they returned to their country of origin. Included in this group were the overwhelming majority of Jewish Holocaust survivors. These were the people for whom Eleanor Roosevelt was fighting. In the end she prevailed. The UN Assembly adopted her view and declared that refugees would have a choice about where to settle. This was a key decision for the Jews in the DP camps.

The great majority of them had originally lived in countries with long histories of anti-Semitism. Aware of this, Harrison had ended his report by pointing out that "the civilized world owes it to this handful of survivors to provide them with a home where they can again settle down and begin to live as human beings."[19] Harrison had reported that the DPs overwhelmingly wanted to go to Palestine (the future State of Israel). In a subsequent poll of 19,000 Jewish DPs, 97 percent named Palestine as their preferred destination. Asked to pick a second choice, many of them wrote "crematorium."[20]

Breaking the news to these families that they were to be repatriated seemed equivalent to delivering a death sentence.[1]

—Denis Hills, British officer
screening DPs for repatriation

There were many glitches when it came to carrying out the UN declaration giving refugees a choice about where to settle. For Jewish DPs, who were stateless, that choice was limited by the immigration policies of most countries, and mainly by the restrictions placed on settling in Palestine by the British who ruled there. In 1946 the majority of these stateless Jews were not in the DP camps. They were still trapped in Eastern Europe, trying to make their way west.

Some of them were Russian Jews whose families had been wiped out by Russian and Polish Ukrainians in the service of the Nazis. Some were Russian Jews fleeing religious persecution in Communist Russia. Some were Polish, Latvian, Lithuanian, or Estonian Jews who had fled deep into Russia to escape the Holocaust during the war. Some were Jews who had been in hiding, and some were Jews who had fought with partisan units in Poland and other Eastern European countries. Now approximately 250,000 of these Jews were moving toward Central and southern Europe in hopes of escaping the devastation, starvation, and chaos of Eastern Europe.

Hanan Werebejczyk, a Polish Jew who survived Auschwitz, described what it was like: "A general migration was underway in Central Europe. The trains were packed. Forced laborers from Germany were returning to their homelands, to Poland, to the Soviet Union, and to other countries. Jews were traveling in all directions, some returning to Poland, some fleeing from there and on the way to Germany."[2]

Legacy of The Protocols

Some Jewish DPs made their way back to their hometowns in search of family, relatives, friends, or property. They returned fearfully, and with good reason. Professor Aaron Hass, editorial advisor to the journal *Holocaust* and author of many books on the subject, points out that "anti-Semitism was something with which the Jews of the former Austro-Hungarian Empire and countries farther east such as Poland and Romania, were quite familiar. Anti-Semitically charged Fascist groups—the Hlinka Guard of Slovakia, the Utasha of Croatia, the Arrow Cross of Hungary, the Iron Guard of Romania, the Endc of Poland— made up of well-organized cadres sprang up years before the German invasion." Professor Hass also points out how "the bitterness of peasants . . . was skillfully directed onto the Jew" in most Eastern European countries.[3]

Indeed, a viciously anti-Semitic pamphlet called *The Protocols of the Learned Elders of Zion,* which claimed to expose a Jewish plot to conquer the world and enslave Christians, was specifically written in 1903 at the order of the Russian czar. Its purpose was to redirect peasant violence against the wealthy aristocratic landowners from them to the Jews. *The Protocols* were translated into German, French, English, and many other languages. They not only sparked pogroms (attacks on Jews) in Russia, but encouraged violent anti-Semitism to escalate throughout all of Europe. Now, in the wake of the worst genocide in history, *The Protocols* were being revived and their poison once again spread.

In the aftermath of the Holocaust, there were additional reasons for Jews to be wary of returning home. When they originally fled, or were rounded up and sent to concentration camps, the Nazis had seized their homes, places of business, and other property. However, the Germans had been forced to relinquish what they had taken when they retreated from the Russian army. With no owners in sight, many locals in Eastern European cities and towns simply appropriated the property for themselves and their families. In many villages, where anti-Semitic folklore had long convinced the residents that Jews possessed large caches of gold and jewelry, which they buried, fields were dug up and houses torn down in the search for wealth.

Many of those Jews who returned found their homes and places of business destroyed. Others found families living in their houses and strangers running their stores or factories. However, those who had appropriated their property and would not return it were not always strangers. Often as not they were former neighbors, might even once have been considered friends. Nevertheless, there was no welcome mat out for the returning Jews. A typical greeting was, "What? You came back? They didn't kill all of you?"[4]

The Kielce Massacre

It wasn't just devastating words that greeted returning Jews. Holocaust survivor Ben Helfgott returned to Poland to encounter two Polish officers who held him and his cousin at pistol point and ordered them to stand up against a wall and face execution. They were boys, still in their teens, and eventually the Polish officers relented. "You can consider yourself very lucky," one of them told the youngsters. "We have killed many of your kind. You are the first ones we have left alive." Later, Ben wrote that while he and his cousin had been fortunate, "I cannot help thinking of the many survivors who returned to Poland after the war and who were killed by the Poles."[5]

There were many reasons for Polish anti-Semitism leading to the postwar murder of Jews. There was a long history of Jew hatred fueled by superstition in Poland, particularly in the rural areas. These Poles were poor peasants, and when the German army fled the Russians, the Poles seized property that had once been Jewish. If the Jews were allowed to come back, the Poles might have to return this property. The Poles had themselves been persecuted by the Nazis, and the bitterness they felt often translated into a murderous fury at anything—or anyone—who threatened their shaky postwar status quo. Often they regarded the return of the Jews as just one more invasion that would bring misery just as the invasions of the Germans, and then of the Russians, had. The majority of Poles did not kill Jews, but those who did created a climate of fear among Holocaust survivors.

The best known of such murders occurred in the city of Kielce, Poland, in July 1946. A Christian boy disappeared for three days, and when he returned he claimed to have been kidnapped by Jews. He said he had been held in a cellar where he watched a blood ritual in which "fifteen other Christian children were murdered."[6]

In Kielce the Jews lived in a community building. The boy's story spread and soon some five thousand people surrounded the structure. Polish soldiers went into the building, escorted the Jews out, and turned them over to the mob. Local militia, factory workers, including the director of one factory, and even some members of the clergy took part in the bloodbath that followed. When it was over, forty-one Jews had been killed and sixty injured. Those who died had been slaughtered with axes or clubbed to death.

The killing of returning Jews spread to other cities in Poland. In one Polish village, two young brothers were stoned to death. In another a young Jewish mother was raped and killed.

A plea was made to the bishop of Lublin to make a statement to calm the Catholics of his city. His response was that "the question as to whether or not Jews use [Christian] blood in their rituals has not yet been clarified." The Polish Cardinal Hlond also made a statement. He said that "the fact that their condition is deteriorating is to a great degree due to the Jews themselves."[7] When a Catholic priest in Cracow denounced the riot, he was "forbidden to continue ecclesiastical duties."[8] In other words, he could no longer perform his duties as a priest.

Punishing the Survivors

It should be noted that many Catholics in Poland and elsewhere had helped, hidden, and protected Jews throughout the Holocaust. Priests and nuns in many countries, most notably Italy, had risked their lives and often acted in opposition to Church policy as interpreted by their superiors to save Jews from the slaughter. Nevertheless, there were postwar killings of Jews by both Catholics and Protestants in many countries besides Poland.

In Czechoslovakia there were repeated attacks on German Jews in the capital city of Prague, anti-Jewish demonstrations in Kosice, and a pogrom in Presove in which five Jews were killed. Five Jews who returned to Vilnius, capital of Lithuania, were also murdered. A note pinned to their bodies announced that "this will be the fate of all surviving Jews."[9] In Ischl, Austria, when Jews were attacked by a local mob, a U.S. military court handed down harsh sentences against the mob's ringleaders, causing the Austrian government to protest that the sentence was "contrary to the sentiment of justice of the Austrian population, but is likely to provoke extreme unrest." In Bucharest, Romania, crowds "fell to beating up all the Jews they could lay hands on," using the heavy staffs of Romanian flags as clubs.[10]

On the German side of the German-Polish border, Kurt and Hertha Fuchs had hidden three Jewish boys from the Nazis during the war years. Months after the war ended, local Nazis found out what they had done and shot and killed Kurt Fuchs and one of the young Jews in front of Hertha Fuchs. Forty years later she remembered how she cradled her husband's head in her lap as he lay dying, and how, as the murderers walked away, one of them said, "We can get her now too." But they didn't bother; they just walked away.

The "Greek Bluff"

With a quarter of a million Jews on the move in Europe during this period, and with Jews still being murdered in many countries, the question being asked was what was to become of them? The American and British DP facilities were being filled to overflowing by a constant stream of new arrivals. Where were those still in transit to go? How were they to get there?

No matter where they were heading, refugees frequently had to cross the borders of several countries to reach their destination. This wasn't easy. All of these countries regarded the Jews as stateless people. The countries themselves were in turmoil, and they viewed the Jews as having the potential to add to that turmoil if they crossed their borders. The countries also feared that the Jews might be forced to remain within their boundaries because the next country on the refugees' route might not allow them to cross its borders.

Eventually, the Jews were helped by various Jewish organizations of different countries to reach safe havens. In the beginning, however, it was native Polish and Lithuanian Jews, many of them former partisan fighters, who organized journeys for groups of fellow Jews. They provided forged Red Cross documents and assisted them in fleeing Eastern Europe by train to Berlin, or through Romania to Yugoslavia, or toward Italy. They guided them through mountain passes to unpatrolled borders. They helped them bribe soldiers at guard posts, or provided false passports and other documents, which allowed the Jews to cross the borders.

One escape technique was known as the "Greek bluff."[11] Polish Jews showing documents identifying them as Greeks who had been held in Nazi slave labor camps and were now returning to Greece were permitted to cross the Czechoslovakian border. This ruse was used so often and worked so well that genuine Greeks with authentic documents were arrested by the Czechs because their papers were so different from those the border guards were used to accepting.

The Bricha

As early as October 1945, the first Zionists from Palestine began arriving in Eastern Europe. Zionists were committed to creating a homeland for Jews in Palestine. The Jewish people had originated in the biblical land of Canaan, later known as Palestine and eventually as Israel. Jews had lived there for thousands of years before great numbers of them had fled successive slaughters by both

A Polish woman and her child, who had made their way westward as part of the Bricha, rest on a wooden bunk at the DP shelter at the Rothschild Hospital in Vienna.

Christians and Muslims. Nevertheless, Jews have always lived—albeit at times as a minority—in the land now known as Israel.

Zionism had begun in 1897, a time when Jews were being persecuted throughout Europe, particularly in Poland and Russia. Since the early 1900s, Jews in Europe had begun migrating back to Palestine despite often violent opposition from the Muslim and Christian Palestinian population. Following World War II, that opposition was enforced by the British, who ruled Palestine under a League of Nations mandate and who severely limited Jewish immigration to the country. There were frequent clashes between the British and various Zionist organizations, some of them violent.

Known as *shlichim*, which means emissaries, the Zionists began creating a program for an organized exodus of Jews from Eastern Europe. This program was known as the *Bricha* (Hebrew for "flight"). Its ultimate aim was to bring these stateless Jews to Palestine.

By 1946 the *Bricha* had become "an established organization across much of the [European] continent." The Zionists worked with The Joint, which provided food and clothing for fleeing and often penniless Jewish families, and with members of the Jewish Brigade who had fought with the British against the Nazis in Italy. The Jewish Brigade soldiers transported the refugees in "disguised military trucks, carrying supplies, foiling occupation forces repeatedly."[12]

The Scarlet Pimpernel

One of the most colorful rescuers of the *Bricha* was Yehuda Arazi, nicknamed "The Scarlet Pimpernel" after the elusive revolutionary hero of French fiction. Arazi had been born in Poland and migrated with his family to Palestine when he was sixteen years old. He enlisted in the Haganah, the Jewish underground army in Palestine. He became a secret agent for the Haganah and joined the British police force in Palestine to penetrate their intelligence network. As a double agent, Arazi smuggled arms to the Haganah and helped Jews in Poland, the

Balkans, and North Africa to escape to Palestine. In 1945 the British uncovered his deception. When Arazi escaped, they offered a large reward for his capture.

While the British were still searching for him, Arazi surfaced in Italy wearing the uniform of an officer in the British army. The postwar Italian economy was in turmoil, and the British military, as Arazi put it, was "slack and unbuttoned."[13] Arazi plunged into the black market, swapping goods for services and vice versa. His goal was to use his profits to bring Eastern European Jews to Italy where they might board ships, which would smuggle them into Palestine. A carton of American cigarettes went for $150 on the black market; two packs served to bribe many a border guard to look the other way while a group of Jews slipped into his country.

Arazi made contact with a company of the Jewish Brigade stationed in Milan. They had vehicles, which could be used to transport refugees who had crossed the northern borders of Italy to the coast. Arazi had soldiers of the Jewish Brigade give him their weekly ration of whiskey for the "liquor bank" he drew on to buy black-market food and supplies for the refugees. Concerned that the refugee ships might fall prey to mines left over from the war, Arazi "persuaded the Italian Admiralty Office at Taranto to accept a case of whiskey in trade for a detailed map of the minefields along the coast of Italy."[14]

The Phantom Army

When the British high command sent the Jewish Brigade to North Africa to be demobilized, Arazi lost access to forty trucks used for transporting refugees. He reacted with an ingenious scheme. He created a "phantom army unit," forged requisition papers, and set up a new operation in a large courtyard in Milan.[15] He persuaded the Haganah leadership to smuggle soldiers of the demobilized Jewish Brigade back to Milan to staff his phantom army. He set up military police (MP) signboards, guard posts, and a facility to produce all the documents he needed to satisfy the British that this was a legitimate army operation.

Then, issuing phony papers, Arazi requisitioned a fleet of new vehicles. These not only transported refugees up and down the coast of Italy, but their drivers also used forged orders for clothing and provisions to provide for those sailing to Palestine. The British were increasingly furious at their inability to stop the operation, which was putting Jews on ships illegally bound for Palestine. But British Intelligence never guessed that Yehuda Arazi and his confederates were in plain view, wearing British uniforms in the center of Milan, and behaving like well-disciplined British officers. As two of Arazi's men who later became historians observed, "The sheep were hiding in wolf's clothing."[16]

For many of the fleeing refugees, Arazi's operation was the end of the line in Europe with a homeland of their own almost within their grasp. By the time they reached Italy, they would have crossed many borders, trudged over mountains, forded streams, fought the bitter cold of winter and the melting snows of spring. Escorted by young and able *shlichim,* family groups of children, old people, sick people, and even pregnant women braved every difficulty to reach their goal. They were determined to reach Palestine, which they called "*Eretz Israel—* the place where they don't kill the Jews."[17]

THE POLITICAL STRUGGLE

5

The most shocking fact about the plight of these displaced persons is not that they are interned. It is the fact that the United States Government and people have the means to open the door for many of them but have not done so.[1]

—*Life* magazine,
September 23, 1946

Many nations share the shame of the United States in having refused sanctuary to stateless Jewish survivors following World War II. In most of these countries, including the United States, the restrictive immigration policies had at least a partial basis in anti-Semitic and racist theories with more than a passing resemblance to those advanced by the Nazis. In the United States such policies were achieved by a series of immigration quota bills passed between 1882 and 1929.

Bigoted Quotas

The 1882 act, known as "the Chinese exclusion law," barred Chinese from emigrating to the United States. In 1917 the law was extended to bar people from Southeast Asia. On May 19, 1921, Congress established a quota limiting immigration to "three percent of each nationality that lived in America in 1910." This meant that "Russians, Italians and Greeks" were to be "admitted at one-fifth their previous number."[2] In 1924 the quota for each nationality was lowered to 2 percent. In 1929 a "national origins formula placed the maximum" of people allowed to enter the United States each year "at approximately 154,000."[3] This was less than one-fifth of the number of immigrants each year prior to World War I.

As a result of these restrictions, the Jews of Eastern Europe were faced with a yearly immigration quota one-sixth that of people from Western Europe who used only one-fourth of their quota. Also, the Eastern European quota lumped Jews and non-Jews together. In effect, the Eastern European Holocaust survivors were little better off than the refugees of war-torn China who had no quota at all. Nor did the annual quota affecting Jews carry over from one year to the next. The fact that it went unfulfilled during the war did not alter the immigration quota after the war.

"Be Quiet, Jews"

In 1938, before the war began, an international conference to consider the plight of refugees was held at Evian in France on the shores of Lake Geneva. At that time Jews were already fleeing Nazi persecution in Germany, Hungary, Austria, Romania, and other countries. The Japanese invasion of China and the Italian invasion of Ethiopia had also created large refugee populations.

Thirty-two nations sent representatives to the Evian Conference. They "stood up, one by one, to explain why they could not accept refugees."[4] The position voiced by Myron C. Taylor, the U.S. representative and chairman of the conference, was basically no different from that of the representatives of the other nations. Playwright Ben Hecht captured the bitterness of Jews trapped by these positions in a long poem with this refrain:

> Hang and burn, but be quiet, Jews,
> The world is busy with other news.[5]

President Roosevelt, Harry Truman's predecessor, had seemingly turned a deaf ear to the problem of Jewish refugees both prior to the war and—with one exception—after it started. According to foreign correspondent Ruth Gruber, who had also served as an assistant to Roosevelt's Secretary of the Interior,

Harold Ickes, during the war, "changes in the quota were unthinkable. The labor unions were opposed, fearing the refugees would take their jobs." The excuse was made that "it's Congress and the State Department who bar refugees. Roosevelt can't act alone. He can't have his New Deal labeled the Jew Deal."[6]

The St. Louis Tragedy

This was the background to a shameful incident that took place in 1939, a few months before World War II began. A deal was made between a German steamship company and an official of the Cuban government to provide false visas to Jewish refugees, which would enable them to sail to and remain in Cuba. The refugees, who paid for both their steamship fare and the visas, didn't know the visas were false. On May 13, 930 Jews sailed out of Hamburg on the liner *St. Louis,* bound for Havana. Among them were 737 Jews with quota numbers, which made them eligible to enter the U.S. from Havana within one to three years.

When the *St. Louis* reached Havana on May 27, the Cuban government refused to honor the false visas. The Jews were not permitted to go ashore. The ship was ordered to leave Havana harbor with its Jewish passengers.

The captain of the *St. Louis,* Gustave Schroeder, was a German anti-Nazi with the greatest respect and sympathy for his Jewish passengers. He sailed his ship to the Florida coast, steaming back and forth in the hopes that appeals by Jewish groups in the United States to allow him to land his passengers would be honored by the U.S. government. That didn't happen. Instead, "the United States Coast Guard ordered the vessel out of American territorial waters, and a cutter followed closely behind to ensure that no refugee jumped overboard to swim ashore."[7]

Captain Schroeder radioed Berlin asking permission to take the Jews to Shanghai. Permission was denied. Ordered to return to Europe, he proceeded at the slowest possible speed. A watchdog committee to prevent suicides was formed by the Jews aboard the *St. Louis*. Finally, Captain Schroeder received permission to bring the Jews to England, Belgium, France, and the Netherlands. The 287 Jews who landed in England were herded into internment camps. The 621 who disembarked in Europe were captured by the Nazis within 12 months. All but 4 of them died in the Holocaust.

"Another Concentration Camp"

The British were not the only ones who herded refugee Jews into internment camps. The United States also did. The occasion was the one rescue effort that took place under the Roosevelt administration. It happened in 1944 when the war in Europe had been going on for almost five years and would continue for another year before it was finally won.

On June 12, 1944, President Roosevelt read a message to Congress. He told them that "this nation is appalled by the systematic persecution of helpless minority groups by the Nazis," adding that "the fury of their insane desire to wipe out the Jewish race in Europe continues undiminished."[8] He also announced that a "'temporary haven' was being prepared at a former army barracks in Oswego, New York," for one thousand refugees.[9]

Considering the hundreds of thousands of Jews still at risk of slaughter by the Nazis, the rescue of one thousand was more a statement of humanitarianism than a full-fledged program to save Jews from the ongoing Holocaust. Three thousand Jews applied to go to the "temporary haven." However, of the 982 refugees permitted to set out for Oswego, only 874 were Jewish. "Roosevelt," according to Ruth Gruber, "had cautioned that the camp not be known as a Jewish camp; he wanted refugees of all denominations."[10]

When the refugees reached Oswego, they were taken to Fort Ontario. Here they were herded into a fenced compound guarded by military police. One of the Jewish refugees, Arthur Hirt, summed up their reaction: "It's another concentration camp!" he declared.[11]

"Inhumane and Wasteful"

For the next year the refugees were confined in the Fort Ontario camp. Then, on July 6, 1945, two months after the war ended, the House Immigration and Naturalization Committee recommended that the Department of State and the Department of Justice look into the question of "returning the refugees to their homeland." If they were reluctant to go, then they should be declared "illegally present in the country" and the attorney general should "undertake deportation proceedings," according to the House Committee recommendation.[12]

The prospects for the refugees held in Fort Ontario were grim, but then, on December 22, 1945, the matter was taken out of the hands of Congress and the various government departments by President Truman. He had decided that "it would be inhumane and wasteful to require these people to go all the way back to Europe merely for the purpose of applying there for immigration visas and returning to the United States." Therefore, Truman announced, he was "directing the Secretary of State and the Attorney General to adjust the immigration status of the members of this camp who may wish to remain here."[13]

On January 17, 1946, the first three busloads of refugees were allowed to leave the camp. They were taken to Niagara Falls where a government representative presented each of them with an American visa decorated with a red seal and a ribbon. They were now in the country legally, able to travel wherever they wished, and free to become future American citizens.

The Palestine Initiative Fails

In his statement making the Oswego refugees eligible for United States citizenship, President Truman did not ask Congress to change the highly restrictive immigration quotas affecting the Jewish DPs trapped in Europe. However, he did follow through on the recommendation of the Harrison Report that "100,000 Jews . . . be allowed to enter Palestine." Since the British ruled in

Palestine, "Truman contacted the British Prime Minister, Clement Atlee, with the recommendation."[14]

Atlee responded that such a mass migration would "set aflame the whole Middle East."[15] His reaction reflected a common fear, widespread in both Great Britain and America, that the Arab nations might retaliate against allowing such a large number of Jews to emigrate to Palestine by cutting off supplies of oil to both nations. Nevertheless, it was agreed that an Anglo-American Committee of Inquiry to investigate the status of DPs should be appointed. The committee's recommendation, issued in April 1946, agreed with the Harrison report that 100,000 Jews be allowed into Palestine.

Atlee rejected the recommendation and proclaimed that no more than 1,500 Jews would be allowed to migrate to Palestine each month. This quota of 18,000 a year continued until the British rule in Palestine ended in 1948. When Truman repeatedly suggested increasing the quota, British Foreign Secretary Ernest Bevin sneered that "they do not want too many of them [Jews] in New York."[16]

Behind the Closed Door Policy

The city of New York had the largest Jewish population of any city in the world. It had always been a traditional haven for all those fleeing the tyranny and poverty of other lands. New Yorkers on the whole would not have agreed with Bevin, but in other parts of the United States there was still very strong feeling against increasing immigration quotas. According to the United States Displaced Persons Committee's Report, "the Veterans of Foreign Wars, the American Legion, and other groups with like views presented a solid front of opposition to plans for [increased] immigration, and their position was reflected editorially in the *Chicago Tribune*."[17]

The Washington Post pointed out the hypocrisy of the United States's position. "We have exhorted the British to admit a considerable number of them [Jews] to Palestine," they editorialized. "Yet we have done nothing on our own

Jewish DPs in a German camp demonstrate for a policy of free immigration to Palestine.

account to afford refuge to them here." As late as February 1947, a year and a half after the war had ended, the Catholic journal *Commonweal* warned that there was "an organized campaign against permitting the entrance of displaced persons into the United States." *Commonweal* also reported that "the President's mail was seven to one against admission."[18]

Truman had to weigh this anti-immigration public opinion backed up by congressional opposition to easing quotas against a DP situation in Europe, which was growing worse by the day. According to estimates by Jewish refugee organizations, "at the end of 1946 the number of Jewish DPs was estimated at 250,000, 185,000 of whom were in Germany, 45,000 in Austria, and 20,000 in Italy." There had been a major change in "the demographic composition of the DP population." Now "the DPs were largely Jews from Eastern Europe, primarily Poland." There were also "a large number of family units and children" who had fled from Communist Russia. Most of the heads of the refugee organizations believed that President Truman continued to be personally interested in this problem, but was unable to effectively put his policies into action.[19]

The Stratton Bill

Truman's policies changed over the year and a half following the war's end. More and more he was standing up against public opinion and Congress in his battle to open the doors of the United States to Jewish DPs. On January 6, 1947, in his State of the Union message, the president "urged Congress to authorize the admission of displaced persons to the United States." He pointed out that "only about five thousand of them have entered this country since May 1946." He urged Congress to enact legislation that would admit "thousands of homeless and suffering refugees of all faiths" to the United States.[20]

On April 1, 1947, Republican congressman William Stratton of Illinois introduced a bill to authorize the admission of 100,000 DPs a year for four years.

Secretary of State George C. Marshall and Attorney General Tom Clark spoke out in favor of the bill. Secretary of War Robert W. Patterson also supported it, pointing out that "sixty percent of the displaced persons in Europe were being cared for by the American government" in DP camps at a cost of $100 million per year.[21]

Opponents of the Stratton bill claimed that the United States had already done enough for the refugees and should not be required to provide further assistance. The effect of relaxing immigration quotas on the labor market was again cited, and it was pointed out that there was a housing shortage with not enough low-cost units available for World War II veterans. The charge was also repeatedly made that the DPs were "degenerates, criminals and subversives . . . whose only thought was to come to the United States to spread Communism or other unwanted doctrines."[22]

By now the American Federation of Labor and the Congress of Industrial Organizations had changed their position. Along with the U.S. Department of Labor, they stated that the increase in immigration would not "cause any undue competition for jobs."[23] The Federal Housing Administration testified that passing the Stratton bill would not seriously affect the housing situation. Despite all the arguments, however, the Stratton bill died in committee after nine months of discussion.

Senate Bill S.2242

While the House of Representatives was still stalling on the Stratton bill, President Truman sent Congress another message. On July 7, 1947, he reminded them that the United States had been "founded by immigrants, many of whom fled oppression and persecution." Truman impressed upon the legislators that there was an "urgent need for action."[24] Nineteen days later the Senate passed a resolution to appoint a committee to assess the DP situation and make recommendations on what to do about it. The result was *Displaced Persons in Europe,* a report which led to the introduction of a bill that would be known as S.2242.

Those who favored increasing immigration quotas found the bill "discriminatory and inadequate." Its recommendations were based on 1945 DP figures, which had since tripled. This had the effect, said the bill's opponents, of discriminating against "Jewish as well as Catholic refugees" who had only managed to reach the DP camps in 1946 and 1947. The bill set a new quota good for only two years—50,000 in 1949 and 50,000 in 1950. There were many additional restrictions on those who would be permitted to enter.

There were amendments to S.2242, most of which amounted to only minor adjustments. The only real improvement as far as DPs were concerned was an increase in the number to be admitted, from 100,000 to 200,000. Nevertheless, at the beginning of June 1948, after eleven and a half hours of continuous debate, the Senate passed the bill by a vote of 63 to 13.

The New York Times called the DP bill "a sorry job," adding that "every liberalizing amendment which would have treated DPs equally as members of the human race . . . was voted down." The editorial concluded that "the Senate bill in its present form ought not to be put on the statute books." President Truman said that sections of the bill "form a pattern of discrimination and intolerance wholly inconsistent with the American sense of justice." Nevertheless, on June 25, 1948, he signed S.2242 into law. "I have signed this bill in spite of its many defects," he explained, "in order not to delay further the beginning of a resettlement program."[25]

The Unkept Promise

Altogether, during the five to seven years immediately following the war, 400,000 refugees were admitted to America. About a third of them—137,000—were Jews. Some Eastern European Jews also found new homes in the Scandinavian countries, France, Canada, Britain, and Israel. The two countries in which the most Jewish refugees settled were the United States and Israel.

Prior to Israel's independence in 1948, most Jews sailed illegally to what was then Palestine and were smuggled into the country.

Children orphaned by the war, Jews and Christians alike, were given priority to emigrate to the U.S. For other Jewish DPs, U.S. visas were harder to obtain. Truman continued to fight intermittently to have the quotas eased, and he did have some small successes. Many of those who fought for admission of the Jewish DPs regarded him as a great champion of their cause. Some activists, however, regarded him as too conciliatory in his balancing of the plight of the DPs against practical politics at home and the demands of diplomacy abroad.

Historian Leonard Dinnerstein tends to agree with them. He believes the efforts made by the United States did not meet the needs of the Jewish refugees in Europe, who were often denied the opportunity to find new homes and new lives. Dinnerstein writes that "strong national prejudices, procrastination in Congress, and some less than dynamic leadership from the White House combined to prolong the miseries of those Jews who survived the Holocaust."[26]

Those Jews did not receive the welcome promised in the poem by Emma Lazarus inscribed on the Statue of Liberty in New York harbor:

Give me your tired, your poor,
Your huddled masses yearning to breathe free,
The wretched refuse of your teeming shore,
Send these, the homeless, tempest-tossed, to me:
I lift my lamp beside the golden door.[27]

In the days following the end of the war, the lamp was dimmed, the door too often closed.

REVIVAL OF HOPE

6

An armed German policeman, who had lived his adult life under the Nazi regime, cruelly and cowardly and in cold blood, murdered an unarmed, poor, unfortunate, defenseless Jew. There was no reason for it.[1]

—Fiorello LaGuardia,
director general of UNRRA

On March 29, 1946, without informing the U.S. military authorities who were in charge of the Jewish DP camp at Stuttgart, German police entered the camp with trained police dogs to search for black-market goods. When the DPs protested, shouting, one of the officers shot and killed a Jewish concentration camp survivor. As a result of the incident, German police were forbidden to enter the DP camps unless accompanied by a U.S. or British officer, and were forbidden to bring guns in with them.

Both official and unofficial attitudes in Germany and Austria where most of the Jewish DP camps were located became increasingly hostile. With the flow of Eastern European refugees bringing the total of Jews in Germany by the end of 1946 to 185,000 and mounting, resentment at Allied efforts to rehabilitate the DPs grew. Reacting to pressures resulting from the Harrison Report, and disregarding Cold War policy designed to conciliate the Germans, some of the Allied actions were inconsistent, clumsy, and ill conceived. In Munich, 10,000 Germans were evicted from their homes to create housing for the DPs. German war veterans were transferred from hospitals to make way for DP patients. German animosity was understandable, if not—in light of the Holocaust—excusable.

There were many other actions favoring DPs and adversely affecting Germans and Austrians. However, not all of the DPs involved in them were Jews. A good many were refugees from other countries who had fled the

Russians. Some were even among the 12 million *Volksdeutschen* (Germans who had lived in Czechoslovakia) forced to flee to Germany after the war. Nevertheless, many Germans believed that the refugees who were unfairly favored by Allied military occupation policy were Jews. Years of Nazi propaganda had conditioned them to hold the Jews responsible.

The Cold War Dilemma

Sometimes these anti-Semitic attitudes rubbed off on the American soldiers who came in contact with the DPs. In his book on displaced persons, Professor Mark Wyman describes how the inexperienced American soldiers who replaced the wartime troops "transferred their dislike of Germans to the DPs." This was also true of officers who "soon discovered that the former Nazi officials at least knew how to address an officer and could help the Americans locate good houses, liquor and women. And so the local U.S. army colonel's secretary was a former SS girl, and a former SS trooper in the district got rich on illegal sales and purchases, made possible by helping Americans in black market deals. Similarly, Americans in charge of construction crews favored German POWs as workers over DPs or Italian POWs; the Germans were 'generally industrious, obedient and well-behaved.' . . . American soldiers . . . found it difficult to square the image of a bloodthirsty Nazi with the neat, clean, orderly world they found among Germans. DPs seemed less desirable."[2] A 1946 poll of occupying American troops revealed that 22 percent believed that "the Germans had good reason to distrust the Jews."[3]

Such attitudes led to many confrontations between occupation soldiers and DPs. Some were violent. When American soldiers assigned to the Bleidern DP camp in Ansbach, Germany, allegedly beat up two Holocaust survivors, an angry mob of Jewish DPs retaliated. They waded into a group of U.S. servicemen and kidnapped two of them. It took a squad of U.S. troops to rescue the soldiers later.

Hostility from American occupation forces toward DPs may have reflected the change in attitude at the top. Russia, now occupying much of Eastern Europe, including East Germany, was seen as an aggressor bent on spreading Communist rule over all of Europe. By the summer of 1946, the United States regarded Russia as a potential enemy. The possibility of a new war hung over the Continent and affected the situation of the DPs. When UNRRA argued for improved conditions and care for the DPs, General Lucius Clay, who after General Eisenhower left became American high commissioner for Germany, responded that his job was "to reconstitute the German economy without delay."[4]

According to Professor Wyman, "this was the dilemma: Punish the Germans, or help them? Ferret out ex-Nazis or hire them? Block the fraternization of soldiers with Germans, or urge the troops to organize youth clubs so German young people could learn democratic ways?"[5]

DP Culture Clashes

These were not questions for Holocaust survivors. Anti-German feelings among many of them would last the rest of their lives. As Alexander Pechersky, a Russian Jew who organized an escape from the Sobibor death camp put it, "we must live in order to take our revenge."[6] Pechersky himself lived to testify in the war crimes trial of twelve Nazis. Ten of the twelve were judged guilty and hanged.

Some Jews defined revenge differently. Dr. Samuel Gringauz, president of the Council of Liberated Jews in the American zone, told a group of young survivors that "not even the devil has prepared a revenge fitting for the spilled blood of a little child. Your children, the carriers of our revenge, must find revenge in existence."[7]

For most Jewish DPs, however, there were more immediate problems than revenge of any sort. By 1947 there were more internment camps for Jews than other DPs. The International Refugee Organization (IRO) took over from

UNRRA to run them, subject to military authority. The camps were very over-crowded due to the influx of Jews from Eastern Europe. These DPs came from a variety of places—the Ukraine, Poland, Latvia, Lithuania, Hungary, Romania, and others—and spoke a variety of languages. As many as a dozen tongues were sometimes spoken in one DP dormitory. This made communication among the DPs difficult. Along with culture clashes, this sometimes led to misunderstandings and even violence.

While there was still apathy and despair among the original DPs, the new arrivals were different. They had fought, connived, bribed, and gone through incredible hardship to reach the American zones of Austria and Germany. They had survived by being aggressive. The hardship they had endured had not made some of them upright citizens. Sometimes they equated fighting, stealing, and cheating with survival. As one Eastern European concentration camp survivor, still a child, put it: "I survived because I was strong enough to snatch food from people who were too weak to keep it."[8]

The Camps Become Communities

The problem of keeping order, along with a variety of other problems, was solved by the Jewish DPs themselves. Inmates at each camp elected a committee to administer it. Money for various activities in the camps was provided by The Joint and other Jewish agencies. With their help, the camps' DP administrations assumed responsibility for keeping order, punishing thieves and other malefactors, maintaining high standards of hygiene and sanitation, and setting up facilities for cultural activities and religious services.

Surmounting many difficulties, schools were established in the camps. With help and support from former Jewish Brigade soldiers, the Palestine Jewish community, and a variety of welfare agencies, the network of DP camp schools grew rapidly. Despite all of the problems and shortcomings of space and supplies, dedicated teachers and instructors from inside and outside the camps built a successful educational system. At the same time, they coped with the mental and emotional problems of the children (many of them orphans) of the Holocaust.

Once they were organized, the Jewish DPs began taking an active interest in the politics they blamed for keeping them in the camps. They published more than seventy newspapers, most in Yiddish, but some in Hebrew. These were the two languages that most DPs had in common. They also established the *Tsentraler Historisher Komisiye* (Central Historical Commission), which gathered material to be used in trying and convicting Nazi war criminals.

The Zionist Solution

It was an American journalist, I. F. Stone, who at one point during the development of programs in the Jewish DP camps defined the three groups who made up their populations. The first group, a minority, consisted of "people who had been hurt morally by the things they had to do to survive. Among them were black marketeers and petty speculators. A second group was made up of those who had little stamina left. . . . It was hard to get them to do much of anything." The third group was composed of "people of natural leadership and ability who organized schools and workshops and helped to train their fellows for a useful life elsewhere. Almost all of them wanted to go to Palestine."[9]

Zionists—mostly from Palestine, but also from the United States and elsewhere—were increasingly active in the camps. They set up programs, provided funding, and organized the Jewish DPs under the Hebrew name *She'erit ha-Pletah* (surviving remnant). A variation of the name—*Sharit Ha-Plita*—headed the lists of survivors compiled by the Zionists and circulated among the camps to aid the DPs in reestablishing contact with loved ones who had survived the Holocaust. The Zionists viewed the DP problem as "part and parcel of the Zionist struggle for the immigration of Jews to Palestine and for the establishment of a Jewish state there."[10]

They were frankly determined to convert the Jewish DPs to Zionism, an effort which drew criticism from some Jews and non-Jews. One notable opponent was Lessing Rosenwald, an anti-Zionist American Jew who formed the Citizens Committee for Displaced Persons in an effort to increase Jewish immigration to the United States as an alternative to Palestine. Despite efforts by chapters of the committee in thirty-eight states, the campaign failed.

In the DP camps, the Zionists were extremely successful in pushing their program of emigration to Palestine as the only realistic solution for stateless Jews. According to The Joint worker Koppel Pinson, Zionists "were the only ones that had a program that seemed to make sense after this catastrophe." He explained that "emotionally and psychologically as well as in a real physical sense," Palestine and salvation became one and the same to the Jewish DPs.[11] The Zionist message replaced post-Holocaust depression with hope.

One DP who had been converted to Zionism put it this way: "I'm a Jew. That's enough. We have wandered enough. We have worked and struggled too long on the lands of other peoples. We must build a land of our own."[12]

The Moral of the Bulrushes

Zionism was not a religious movement. Indeed, prior to the Holocaust, many Jews had opposed Zionism. Some of this opposition was religious in nature. Some Orthodox Jews believed it was heresy to establish a Jewish homeland before the Messiah came and decreed its existence. Other Jews believed in assimilating within the countries in which they lived. This was particularly true of German Jews before the Nazis rose to prominence, and of Jews in the United States before the horrors of the Holocaust commanded their attention. The Jews in the DP camps who embraced Zionism did not necessarily become more religious, but rather more accepting of Jewish tradition. Through Zionism they found pride in that tradition.

Nevertheless, there was no effort made to separate that tradition, nor

Zionism itself for that matter, from religion. Jews who once might have argued over their various points of view had been united by the Holocaust and now found common ground in the rearing and education of the DP children. The children were, in all eyes, the post-Holocaust Jewish future. Non-Zionist religious movements such as *Agudat Israel* and *Po'alei Agudat Israel* were active in the DP camps. "Surviving teachers and students in two of the famous Yeshiboth (seminaries) of Poland, the Lubovitcher and the Lubliner, were transported en masse to the camps."[13] One camp had a yeshiva where fifty students were studying to be rabbis. Thus Jewish sects opposed to Zionism worked alongside Zionists to educate the children.

In one class the difference between DP children and other children was highlighted by the response to the story of Moses being abandoned in the bulrushes by his mother. The question was raised as to whether a mother could—or should—do such a thing. Yes, said the children. They had seen mothers tossing children out of trains to save them from the death camps. Some of the children in the camp had been given away to strangers—non-Jews—in the hope that they would survive. Moses' mother, it was concluded, had acted to save her baby from an Egyptian death sentence.

Although non-Zionists were active, it was Zionism that was the driving force behind the expansion of the educational systems in the camps. Some of the systems ran from preschool through college. At the Jewish DP camp in Landsburg, Germany, over seven hundred teens were training to be carpenters, electricians, auto mechanics, tinsmiths, nurses, tailors, dressmakers, and for other skilled occupations.

The Zionists viewed the schools as "the main instrument for preparing the youth for immigration to Palestine."[14] Toward this end, they persuaded the military authorities to requisition farms where young people might receive the agricultural training that would be so necessary to make the desert bloom once Palestine became Israel. Some orphans who had received such training were already being smuggled into Palestine.

"Alone Together"

Initially, many survivors who had been starved and beaten while being cruelly overworked in the Nazi camps refused to do any work in the DP camps. The Zionist dream changed that. Now they eagerly worked to learn and practice new skills, which would help to build a Jewish state in Palestine.

Apathy was banished in other ways as well. While enduring the hardships and malnutrition of the concentration camps, some women prisoners had stopped menstruating. Now, with improved diet and health, they began to menstruate again. Some DPs, women and men alike, experienced a revival of sexual interest. For most—particularly those who had lost their families in the Holocaust—it was not so much sex as a desperate need to establish new relationships, to build new family structures, to have children—Jewish children to replace those who had been murdered.

There were "wholesale weddings" in the camps, according to one woman who was married there, but wished to remain anonymous. Within a year after the war's end, Jewish DPs in the Bergen-Belsen camp were marrying at the rate of twenty weddings a day. The total number of weddings in all the camps by the end of 1946 was running as high as one thousand per month. Most Jewish DPs married other DPs. It was difficult for them to relate intimately with someone who had not known horrors similar to the ones they had known.

The marriages were not always love matches. The fear of loneliness and the need for closeness motivated many marriages in the camps. One DP who had lost his family proposed to another with these words: "I am alone. I have no one, I have lost everything. You are alone. You have no one. You have lost everything. Let us be alone together."[15]

A Soaring Birthrate

Although freedom and survival brought a rebirth of sexuality to some, many DPs "felt sexually insecure throughout their adult life."[16] The sexual growth and

A double wedding at the Feldafing DP camp in Germany, 1945

experience of adolescence had been denied many of them by the awful pressures of the death camps. Older DPs who had lost wives or husbands that they loved found passion difficult to come by with new mates.

Despite this, "by the end of 1946 . . . nearly 1,000 babies were being born each month" in the Jewish DP camps.[17] Indeed, the DP camps had the highest birthrate of any Jewish community in the world at that time. Entire camp populations would rejoice at these births, just as they had turned out for the weddings.

It was as if, without planning it, the Jews were having children to prove that Hitler hadn't won. Despite the Nazi genocide, the Jewish people would not cease to exist. They would have children and rear them in a homeland of their own. This was the promise of Zionism. As a banner in one DP camp proclaimed:

WE DEMAND TO OPEN THE GATES OF PALESTINE![18]

I believe that full support of the so-called illegal immigration is a moral obligation for world Jewry and a Christian duty for its friends. I believe that the only hope lies in filling the waters of Palestine with so many illegal boats that the pressure on the British and the conscience of the world becomes unbearable. And if those ships are illegal, so was the Boston Tea Party.[1]

—Journalist I. F. Stone reporting on the smuggling of DPs into Palestine in 1946

In August 1945, less than three months after World War II ended in Europe, the first postwar boatload of illegal immigrants bound for Palestine left from a remote port on the southern coast of Italy. The vessel was a 25-ton fishing boat named *Dalin*. It carried 35 Jewish DPs from a variety of European countries. It traveled 2,500 miles (4,000 kilometers) and successfully smuggled its passengers into Palestine. The *Dalin* then returned to its Italian base to take on more Jews for another voyage.

Over the next 3 years, 66 ships carried 70,000 illegal immigrants to the shores of Palestine. Two of the ships sailed from North Africa, the rest from Europe. Forty sailed from Italy and most of the others from Greece. The bribing of officials, a general anti-British feeling, and sympathy for the DPs resulted in a great deal of cooperation from the Italians and the Greeks.

From Greece to Palestine

Spiro Gaganis, a Greek from Athens, served as a liaison between the *Bricha* and the maritime suppliers in Greek ports. The *Bricha* would shepherd the DPs from camps, or from Eastern Europe, to embarkation points. Gaganis would procure ships and supplies and sometimes even crews for their journeys.

They called him "the Goose" because of the smooth and silent way he functioned.[2] On one occasion he bought a 200-ton boat meant to carry forty passengers and had it rebuilt to carry two hundred. Gaganis bribed port officials to look the other way, and the fully loaded boat set sail for Palestine. In complete silence, with all lights out, it slipped past the British warships patrolling the coast of Greece.

Off the coast of Palestine they were met by Jews with rowboats. When the boats couldn't carry them all, some of the young men carried the DPs to shore on their backs. Once ashore, the new arrivals were dispersed among various *kibbutzim* (farming cooperatives) to blend into the general population.

Before the operation could be completed, British troops arrived. Eleven of the DPs—a few of them elderly, a few of them children—along with the ship's crew were taken into custody. The crew was later sent back to Greece. The DPs were taken to a main Palestine internment camp at Athlit. In October 1945 soldiers of Haganah raided the Athlit camp and freed most of the inmates.

The Irgun Strikes

The illegal immigration was increasing the Jewish population at a rate alarming to Arab Palestinians. Neighboring Arab states viewed it as a European plot to recolonize the Middle East. On October 20, 1945, Egypt, Syria, Iraq, and Lebanon announced the formation of the Arab League. They warned that "a Jewish state in Palestine would mean war."[3] Conflicts between Jews and Palestinian Arabs mounted.

In June 1946 the British declared martial law in Palestine. They launched a drive against the 80,000-member Haganah, arresting 1,000 people and killing 5. The ferocity of the British action was fueled by the kidnapping of five British officers. The kidnapping had not been the work of the Haganah, but rather of a smaller extremist group of Jewish militants called the Irgun.

Less than a month later, the Irgun struck again, bombing the British government headquarters at the King David Hotel in Jerusalem. More than one hundred people were killed. The attack was led by Menachem Begin, who would one day become prime minister of Israel. According to Begin, "the force of the explosion surpassed all our hopes."[4]

At this point there were 80,000 British troops in Palestine, roughly the same number as the Haganah could muster. The British soldiers, however, were fully armed and equipped with tanks and weapons carriers, as well as being backed up by a British police force of 20,000 men. In addition, there was the British navy with its excellent manpower and equipment—one of the most effective naval forces in the world.

The Fede

Throughout 1946 the British fleet patrolled the waters between the southern coast of Europe and Palestine aggressively and in force. The British were determined that the fleet should enforce Palestine immigration restrictions with the utmost militancy. This led to an incident, which aroused worldwide sympathy for the DPs and embarrassed the British.

The key figure behind the incident, which took place in April and May of 1946, was an old nemesis of the British, "The Scarlet Pimpernel," Yehuda Arazi. Chartering a large vessel, the *Fede,* Arazi obtained an Italian license to carry a cargo of salt from the Italian Riviera to the island of Sardinia. He bribed port authorities to look the other way when human beings were substituted for the salt. However, when trucks carrying a thousand DPs arrived at the docks the Italian police, who had not been bribed, leaped to the conclusion that they were Fascists attempting to flee to Spain. Arazi defused the situation. He gained the sympathy of the police by having the DPs show the concentration camp numbers tattooed on their arms. The anti-Fascist police then allowed them to board the *Fede.*

Meanwhile, British gunboats had received a tip that the *Fede* would be carrying refugees bound for Palestine. The delay the police had caused enabled the British warships to block the port and prevent the *Fede* from sailing. The DPs

Refugees crowd the decks of the Fede upon its arrival at Haifa, Palestine.

were ordered to disembark. When they refused, the British commander announced that the ship would be boarded and the Jews removed by force. Arazi responded that if that was attempted, the ship would be blown up, killing all on board, including any British boarding party.

"The Gate of Zion"

The British did not board the *Fede*. However, they did seal off the port with tanks, and a British warship pulled up alongside the *Fede* with its big guns at the ready. As the ranking British officers were trying to figure out what to do, Arazi went public. He notified the news organizations of the world that a thousand Holocaust survivors were jammed onto a leaky tub, which was under siege by the tanks, guns, and ships of the British navy. Reporters descended on the scene to cover the story. Italians from the surrounding areas also crowded onto the docks.

Arazi got hold of a public-address system and made daily speeches to the crowds, telling them that all Hitler's victims wanted was to go to their new homeland in Palestine. He told the crowd that the DPs were prepared to die before they would leave the ship. Soon the Italians were demonstrating in favor of the Jews. Rocks were thrown, and the British troops were forced to retreat from the docking area. The British called for reinforcements.

With the permission of Italian municipal officials, Arazi put up a sign proclaiming "The Gate of Zion" over the entrance to the port.[5] He flew a Zionist flag alongside the Italian flag above the sign. Then he announced that the DPs had decided to go on a hunger strike. As the days passed into weeks, he announced the number of hours the Jews had gone without food and the number of hunger strikers who had lost consciousness. The story was carried around the world. In Genoa the port workers went on strike in support of the Jews aboard the *Fede*. The Italian prime minister, the admiral of the Italian fleet, and other notables around the world proclaimed sympathy for the hunger strikers.

Arazi warned British prime minister Clement Atlee that if any Holocaust survivors died during the hunger strike their blood would be on his hands. And then Arazi announced that if the ship was not allowed to sail immediately, each day ten DPs would kill themselves on deck in full view of the crowds and journalists gathered on the dock.

The British capitulated and met with Arazi. A truce was arranged. The suicide threat was withdrawn, and the hunger strike was ended. A Seder (feast) to celebrate the Passover holiday was held by the Jews aboard the *Fede.* On May 8, a little more than a month after the originally scheduled departure date of the *Fede,* the British agreed to the immediate admission of all the passengers without regard to the quotas in effect in Palestine. Six weeks later the thousand DPs landed in Palestine.

"Operation Igloo"

Although the British had been embarrassed, the *Fede* incident did not soften their policy regarding illegal immigration to Palestine. On the contrary, they were determined not to let it be a precedent. They stepped up their efforts to stop ships smuggling DPs. During the latter part of 1946 and through 1947 and 1948, they used search planes to spot the vessels, warships to intercept and fire on them, and armed marines to board the ships and subdue the Jews if—as usually happened—they put up a fight. Despite this, there were many successful landings of illegal immigrants in Palestine during this period.

On the other hand, many Jews were taken prisoner on the ships that were intercepted. In August 1946 the British began Operation Igloo, the imprisonment of illegal immigrants on the island of Cyprus.[6] The passengers of captured ships were forced to disembark in Cyprus, where the British operated DP camps alongside prisoner-of-war camps for German soldiers captured during the war. Other Jews who were in Palestine illegally were rounded up by British soldiers and shipped to Cyprus.

Often, Operation Igloo did not go smoothly. In August 1946 a crowd of Palestinian Jews stormed Haifa's barbed-wire port area as illegals were being loaded for deportation. British soldiers opened fire and killed an eighteen-year-old girl. They wounded many others, two of whom died later. As the bullets drove the crowd back, the DPs marching up the gangplank of the ship removing them from Palestine sang the Jewish anthem "Hatikva." In English, *Hatikva* means "hope."

Internment on Cyprus

The detention camps in Cyprus were compounds surrounded by barbed-wire fences patrolled by armed guards. The DPs were quartered in overcrowded tents and Quonset huts. There was no running water or sanitary facilities. The temperature on Cyprus could reach 110 degrees. The sweat and the stench from the open latrines were everywhere.

Captain Rudolph W. Patzert was a non-Jew from the United States who had commanded a ship smuggling DPs into Palestine. He was captured by the British and spent two years in a Cyprus internment camp. Captain Patzert wrote his wife that "the German P. O. W.'s had better accommodations" than the DPs. He had been a merchant marine officer on supply ships braving the German submarine fleet in the North Atlantic during World War II, a harrowing duty with one of the conflict's highest casualty rates. Nevertheless, Captain Patzert said that his imprisonment on Cyprus was the "hardest two years of my life."[7]

Between 1946 and 1949, 52,000 thousand Jews were interned on Cyprus. Approximately 80 percent were between the ages of thirteen and thirty-five. During that time some 2,200 Jewish babies were born in the internment camps. As in the European DP camps, the Jews organized for a future in Palestine. They set up education and job-training centers. Many of the internment camp leaders on Cyprus served as government officials in Israel when it became a nation.

The Exodus

Among the sixty-six ships illegally transporting Jews to Palestine was one known to the British as the *President Warfield*. It had been named after the owner of a United States shipping firm on the Potomac River who had never been president of anything except his company. His daughter was Wallis Simpson, a prominent member of international society who had been twice married and twice divorced. The announcement of marriage plans between her and Britain's King Edward VII had brought on a scandal, which caused him to abdicate the throne. The couple had been Nazi sympathizers. It was ironic that the British named the ship after Ms. Simpson's father. The British navy still called the ship *President Warfield* long after the Zionists renamed it *Exodus*. The name *Exodus* came from the biblical story of the exodus of the Hebrews from the slavery of Egypt to the Promised Land of milk and honey.

The commander of the *Exodus* was Captain Yossi Harel. He had been born in Palestine and joined the Haganah when still a youth. During the 1930s, Yossi Harel had fought against the Arabs. During World War II he had joined the Jewish Brigade and fought with the British against the Nazis. When peace came, he signed on to ferry Holocaust survivors to Palestine. He served on the *Knesset Israel,* sailing from the Yugoslavian coast with a cargo of three thousand DPs. The ship was intercepted by the British and the passengers and crew were sent to Cyprus. Harel escaped and made his way to the small port of Sete, France, where he became captain of the *Exodus.*

On July 11, 1947, the *Exodus* sailed out of Sete with 4,515 Jewish refugees aboard. To get past the French authorities, many of them carried forged visas for South American countries. Others were smuggled aboard the *Exodus* at night in boxes and crates. The intended destination of all was, of course, Palestine.

The Passengers

Aboard the *Exodus,* all the passengers were Jews except one. She was "an elderly Ukrainian woman with a bony face who brought along with her two orphans she had rescued and secretly raised in the spirit of the Jewish faith, in spite of the fact that she hardly knew the difference between its do's and don'ts. . . . The parents had taken the children to her and begged her to save them." An "embittered, childless passenger" who had lost his own children suddenly confronted the Ukrainian woman. He "gazed longingly at the two orphans the woman had raised and cared for . . . and claimed the children were his."[8]

At first some other passengers sided with the man, telling the Ukrainian woman she had no right to protest because "you're not Jewish." Then another passenger who had known the children's parents intervened. She knew they had given their children to the Ukrainian woman. "I saw with my own eyes how their parents were taken away to be killed," she testified. Many of the passengers now supported the Ukrainian woman. The disturbed man backed off, and the question of her right to the children died away. Years later, in Israel, the Ukrainian woman was "officially declared their mother."[9]

The young woman who had spoken up for her was Aliza, who had lost her own family in the Holocaust. Aboard the *Exodus,* Aliza had been drawn to Yosef, an artist whose fiancée had also been murdered during the genocide. When the two decided to marry, there was a celebration. A tentlike shelter on the deck of the *Exodus* had been built by two men from Yosef's hometown city of Vilnius in Lithuania, and now they turned it over to the couple. An old woman contributed candy from a hiding place in the hem of her dress. String was stretched around the shelter and articles of clothing hung over the entrance to shield it from view. Later Yosef threw the paintings he had made of his dead fiancée into the sea. After that he sketched only Aliza, and—from memory— the face of his murdered mother.

Not all the tragedy was in the past. Aboard the *Exodus,* a woman who had survived the horrors of the Holocaust died in childbirth as her husband—also a survivor—knelt by her side. The baby survived the birth, but there was no milk for it. They fed the infant pineapple juice. The baby survived for three months, long enough to be interned in Haifa in Palestine, but then the child died. "Palestine," the baby's father had sobbed when they buried his wife at sea. "Why now?"[10]

Britannia Rules the Waves

As the *Exodus* left the coastal waters of France for the open sea, a British battleship fell in alongside it. Soon there were six British destroyers forming a hostile escort, which more or less surrounded the *Exodus*. They were large, modern ships with long-range cannons. They towered over the *Exodus,* keeping a distance on all sides of about a mile. They would not intercept the ship on the open sea. Action would only be taken when the *Exodus* entered Palestinian waters.

Captain Harel thought he might eventually be able to outrun them, but his first strategy was to try to outwit them. He sailed his ship for the coast of Egypt and then ran parallel to the coast, close enough to it so that the waters would be too shallow for the larger British warships to follow. However, the problem was that setting his Jewish passengers ashore in Egypt, where sympathy ran high for the Palestinian Arabs, was unthinkable. Captain Harel ordered the helmsman to turn the *Exodus* due north and head for the coast of Palestine at top speed.

There were several changes of destination en route, but they were to no avail. Twenty-five miles (40 kilometers) from the Palestinian port of Tel Aviv, the British destroyers closed in, forcing the *Exodus* to come to a halt. British sailors and marines boarded the ship. They were met by immigrants with iron bars, wooden bats, bottles filled with nails and screws, cans of food, and anything else that could be wielded or thrown. The British opened fire, killing three Holocaust survivors and wounding three others.

The *Exodus* was towed to the port of Haifa. Here the British sailors and marines set about forcing the passengers to transfer to three deportation ships. Some of those aboard jumped into the sea and attempted to swim for shore. They were stopped by British police boats, which fired on them. On the deck of the *Exodus,* passengers who didn't move fast enough were being beaten and prodded with billy clubs. Yosef lay on the deck bleeding from a head wound, Aliza's arms supporting him. "My husband is wounded," she pleaded with a British soldier.[11] He responded by striking Yosef again.

At "War With the Jews"

In the end, herded like cattle between rows of British soldiers with drawn bayonets, all but the weakest of the passengers were forced onto the three deportation ships. They assumed they would be taken to Cyprus and held there in internment camps, but they were wrong. The British had decided on a different policy. The illegal immigrants were to be returned to Sete, the port from which they had departed in France.

When the three boats reached Sete, the Jews proclaimed a hunger strike and refused to disembark. The French government said it would not accept any passengers who were forced off the ships against their will. Only 130 passengers who were sick, pregnant, or old agreed to leave the boats in France.

Frustrated, the British sent the three ships with the former *Exodus* passengers to Hamburg, Germany. The plan was to intern them there in former Nazi concentration camps in the British zone of occupation. Two of the three ships were unloaded, but those aboard the third ship refused to disembark. The British forced them off with clubs and high-power hoses. A crowd of Germans gathered to watch the incredible scene of Jews being beaten by those who had so recently won the war against Hitler. As for the Jews, they were now back in the country where the Holocaust began.

Worldwide reaction solidly condemned the British for their handling of the *Exodus* affair. In Britain itself there were protests against the government and the military. Winston Churchill, who had been wartime prime minister of Great Britain but was now out of power, condemned the "callous hostility." He called the policy evidence of the present British government's "war with the Jews."[12]

His Majesty's Government view with favor the establishment in Palestine of a national home for the Jewish people, and will use their best endeavors to facilitate the achievement of this object, it being clearly understood that nothing shall be done which may prejudice the civil and religious rights of existing non-Jewish communities in Palestine.[1]

—The 1917 Balfour Declaration; in 1922 it was
written into the League of Nations mandate
placing Palestine under British control.

Little more than a month after the *Exodus* fiasco, on August 31, 1947, the United Nations Special Committee on Palestine recommended that Great Britain relinquish control of the area granted by the League of Nations in 1922, and that it be partitioned into two states, one Arab and the other Jewish. On November 29 the UN General Assembly authorized the establishment of the two states. The solution was immediately rejected by the head of the Palestine Arab High Committee as "a sort of declaration of war against the Arab countries," which would surely cause "a crusade against the Jews."[2] In Damascus, Syria, angry mobs marched on the Russian, French, and United States embassies—all three countries had voted for partition—and burned their flags. In Palestine, Arabs ambushed two buses and killed six Jews.

At this time, there were roughly a quarter million DPs in the refugee camps of southern Germany and Austria. According to a report by the Hebrew Immigrant Aid Society (HIAS), "two-thirds of the displaced Jews in Germany and Austria are Polish." HIAS pointed out that "the Polish quota is only 6,514 a year" for Jews and non-Jews applying for admission to the United States.[3] Given these restrictions, typical of other countries as well, it is no wonder that those in the DP camps rejoiced so exuberantly at the news that the UN had reaffirmed that the Jews should have a homeland of their own.

It was midnight when word of the UN vote reached the Jewish DP camps in Austria and Germany. All the lights were turned on; the camps were ablaze in the night. The Holocaust survivors "rushed out" of their barracks to the central grounds of the camps and "the singing and dancing went on for hours."[4]

"Operation Deluge"

Some Zionist leaders in Israel and the United States did not share the DPs enthusiasm. The proposed Jewish state would be made up of only 17 percent of Palestinian territory. It was "divided into separate segments, tenuously connected, vulnerable to attack." Furthermore, the British, who for the time being controlled Palestine, had made clear that "there would be no British cooperation in enforcing partition."[5]

The British not only declined to serve as a peacekeeping force between the Arabs and the Jews, but as they prepared to leave Palestine, they turned over their "fortresses and other military installations . . . to the Arabs."[6] They sold weapons to Middle East nations who had pledged to support the Palestinian Arabs. At the same time, laying down laws even as they were getting ready to pull out, the British forbid Jews in Palestine to purchase arms or to organize any sort of fighting force.

During December 1947 and throughout the first half of 1948, confrontations between the British navy and ships smuggling Jews to Palestine increased. The British launched Operation Deluge, a heightened effort "to resist illegal immigration and the Jews fought back against all restrictions."[7] David Ben-Gurion, soon to be Israel's first prime minister, had from the beginning voiced the policy that "the Displaced Persons Camps could be emptied only by the actions of the Jews themselves. They would have to resort to illegal immigration, to defy the British by every means, including force."[8] This determination reached its peak in opposition to Operation Deluge.

Terrorism on Both Sides

As younger DPs were smuggled into Palestine, they became part of the struggle. Some joined the Haganah. At this time it was official Haganah policy to act only in self-defense. They would build up their forces through illegal immigration, and acquire arms and supplies from the black market. Money for this purpose was being donated by Jews and other sympathizers all over the world. In the United States, sympathy for Holocaust survivors ran high and donations to the cause of arms for Israel were particularly generous.

Throughout this period, there was ongoing warfare between Jews and Palestinian Arabs. Despite Haganah's official policy, other Zionist forces did not always act in self-defense. In Haifa they killed eighty-two Arabs, including eight children who died in a bombing. The action was in retaliation for an Arab bombing of a civilian bus station. By mid-January 1948, less than two months after the passing of the UN resolution decreeing partition, skirmishes between Jews and Arabs had claimed two thousand casualties.

There were extremists on both sides. They did not shrink from terrorism. Nor did they always obey the international rules governing warfare. The Arabs laid siege to K'far Etzion, a Jewish settlement not far from Bethlehem. After a long battle in which all but fifteen of the Jews had died fighting, the survivors raised a white flag and surrendered. The Arabs ignored the flag of surrender and killed all fifteen.

The Stern Gang, a Jewish paramilitary force more committed to terrorism than even the extremist Irgun, retaliated with an action designed to panic Palestinians so that they would flee the country. On April 9, 1948, they descended on the Arab village of Deir Yassin. What followed, according to historian and founding president of Brandeis University Abram L. Sachar, was "a massacre that appalled the civilized world and stained Jewish honor for years ahead."[9] More than two hundred villagers, including children, women, and old people were slaughtered. Three days later the Arabs viciously massacred a con-

A Jewish doctor helps a wounded man while a compatriot takes aim from
behind a sandbag wall in a strife-ridden area of Palestine in February 1948.

voy of seventy-seven noncombatant medical personnel—doctors, nurses, faculty, and students—as they were bound for the Hadassah Hospital and the Hebrew University.

Israel Proclaims Statehood

On May 14, 1948, the State of Israel was officially proclaimed by David Ben-Gurion. The next day the British mandate ended, and British troops began the final stages of their withdrawal from Palestine. Recognition of the new state by the United States and Russia came quickly. Great Britain, however, refused to establish diplomatic relations right away. "There is no need to hurry," said one British official.[10]

The Arab League quickly came to the aid of the Palestinians. Five Arab countries declared war on the new nation of Israel. Troops from Syria and Lebanon attacked in the north. Egypt invaded from the south. Armies from Transjordan (now Jordan) and Iraq marched on the new nation of Israel from the east. The coastal road from the new Israeli capital of Tel Aviv to Haifa was cut off by units of the Iraqi army. The highway between Tel Aviv and Jerusalem was captured by Transjordan units. During the first two weeks of independence, Tel Aviv was showered with bombs on a round-the-clock schedule.

Something else also happened during those first two weeks. The British stopped interfering with the emigration of Jewish DPs. Large numbers of Holocaust survivors arrived in Israel from Cyprus and from the camps in Europe. One of the first actions of the new Israeli government was to issue a proclamation inviting all Jews everywhere to join "the struggle for the fulfillment of the dream of generations, the redemption of Israel."[11]

From May through December 1948, an average of 13,500 immigrants arrived on the shores of the new Jewish homeland every month—almost ten times the number allowed under the restrictions that had been imposed by the British. Between the end of World War II and the establishment of the State of

Israel, some 69,000 Jews had either been smuggled into Palestine or captured and interned on Cyprus. Between the birth of Israel and 1951, 331,594 Jews emigrated legally to the new country. Malcolm J. Proudfoot, author of *European Refugees: 1939–1952: A Study in Forced Population Movement,* has speculated that "the state of Israel might not have come into being if other countries had welcomed Europe's Jews earlier."[12] The United States is certainly one of the countries to which he referred.

The Arab-Israeli War

As the war between the invading Arab nations and Israel heated up, it resulted in more and more violence and more and more deaths. In September 1948 the United Nations intervened, sending an official mediator, Count Folke Bernadotte, to the Middle East to try to negotiate between the two sides. Bernadotte concluded that the UN must force a compromise, possibly backed up by UN troops. Insisting on the permanence of "a Jewish state called Israel," he recommended "radical boundary changes, with [the Sea of] Galilee going to Israel and the Negev [Desert] to the Arabs." He proposed "special and separate treatment" for Jerusalem and insisted that "innocent people uprooted from their homes," by which he meant the Palestinian Arabs, must have assurances of their right to return. By the time his report reached the UN, Count Bernadotte, along with another UN representative, had been assassinated in Jerusalem by members of the Stern Gang.[13]

The following month, during a campaign speech for reelection, President Truman vowed that Israel must be "large enough, free enough, and strong enough to make its people self-supporting and secure."[14] This was regarded as a repudiation of the Bernadotte recommendations. It was also, perhaps, a reflection of a new reality in Israel. As the Israeli army swelled with enlistments by new immigrants, the tide of battle had turned in its favor. Many who had survived the Holocaust now gave up their lives in the battle for their new Jewish homeland.

An Israeli counterattack had shattered the Egyptian front. Egyptian supply lines had been cut. The key city of Beersheba had been taken by Israeli forces. In effect, Israel now controlled the Negev. A truce brokered by UN mediator Ralph Bunche had been arrived at between Israel and Egypt. In February 1949 an armistice was signed between Egypt and Israel, which allowed Israel to retain portions of the Negev and left Israeli troops occupying Beersheba. As the Israelis struck with unexpected force against the other Arab armies, Lebanon, Iraq, Syria, and Saudi Arabia signed on to the armistice. In April 1949, Transjordan also agreed to peace.

Although peace had been reached, there was little faith that it would be permanent. None of the members of the Arab League recognized Israel's right to exist as a nation. In May, when the United Nations General Assembly voted to accept Israel as a member, the delegations of Egypt, Iraq, Lebanon, Saudi Arabia, and Yemen walked out of the Assembly Hall in protest. Great Britain, true to form, abstained from voting.

The Palestinian DPs

The reason given by the Arab League nations for their walkout was that Israel had not complied with UN resolutions for the repatriation of Arab refugees and the establishment of an international government in Jerusalem. The argument became valid in December 1949 when Israel launched Operation Jerusalem, the transfer of its national government from Tel Aviv to Jerusalem.[15] In effect, this made Jerusalem the capital of Israel under Israeli, rather than international, jurisdiction.

Efforts to repatriate the Palestinian Arabs who had fled during the war met with limited success. Often, with Israeli government approval, their homes and farms and other property had been taken over by recent Jewish immigrants. Before the establishment of the State of Israel, the Arab population of Palestine had been about 1,319,500. After the Arab-Israeli War, there were only 155,000 Palestinian Arabs left in Israel. Most had been forcibly expelled by the Israelis.

Some had left out of fear due to propaganda circulated by the countries of the Arab League in an effort to portray the Israelis as inhumane. Nevertheless, as Israeli military victories piled up, the Palestinian exodus accelerated. By the end of the war, one million or more Palestinians had fled.

Most of those who departed ended up in refugee camps across the borders of neighboring Arab countries. Over the next fifty years the children who grew up under often horrendous conditions in those camps would be raised to believe that Palestine—now Israel—was their homeland. To this day, hundreds of thousands of Palestinians remain displaced persons.

A Jewish Homeland; a Solution

In a way, the Palestinians were also victims of the Holocaust. The Holocaust had left the Jewish survivors with little choice but to lay claim to a homeland of their own. That this land was Palestine, and that its people became the next mass of displaced persons, was lamentable. It wasn't fair. However, by 1948 the Holocaust and its callous aftermath had pushed the Jews beyond such considerations. As the poem by W. H. Auden points out:

> *I and the public know*
> *What all schoolchildren learn,*
> *Those to whom evil is done*
> *Do evil in return.*[16]

The Holocaust survivors had little choice. The figures tell the story. Six million Jews had been killed in the Holocaust. During the five years following it, migration to those countries that allowed immigration was limited to the following numbers of Jewish survivors: Australia, 4,745; Belgium, 5,000; Brazil, 4,837; Canada, 19,697; France, 8,000; the Netherlands, 5,000; Sweden, 7,200; United Kingdom, 1,000; United States, 105,000.[17]

During the same period, Israel admitted 748,540 Jews.[18] The displaced persons who survived the Nazi genocide had been a problem to most of the countries of the world. To Israel they were Jews returning home. And so, in the eyes of the post-Holocaust world, the problem was solved.

CHRONOLOGY

1945—April—Dachau concentration camp is liberated by American soldiers.

1945—May 8—Germany surrenders; World War II ends in Europe.

1945—June—Jewish Brigade soldiers arrive in the displaced persons (DP) camps.

1945—Summer—President Truman assigns Earl G. Harrison to inspect DP camps.

1945—August—First boatload of illegal Jewish immigrants sails from Italy to Palestine.

1945—August—The Harrison Report is sent to President Truman.

1945—August 31—Truman orders General Eisenhower to make reforms in DP camps.

1945—October 3—Jews in Austrian DP camps stage sit-down strike to protest treatment.

1945—October 8—Eisenhower responds defensively to Harrison Report, then enacts reforms.

1945—October 20—The Arab League is formed.

1946—Eleanor Roosevelt prevails in UN, gaining right for DPs to choose where to settle.

1946—Aided by the *Bricha*, a quarter million Jewish DPs flee persecution in Eastern Europe.

1946—April—The Anglo-American Committee of Inquiry recommends that

100,000 Jewish DPs be allowed to go to Palestine; British prime minister Clement Atlee vetoes the idea.

1946—June—British declare martial law in Palestine.

1946—July—41 Jews are massacred in Kielce, Poland.

1946—July—The Irgun bomb King David Hotel in Jerusalem; more than one hundred people killed.

1946—British limit Jewish immigration to Palestine to 1,500 a month.

1946—August—British institute Operation Igloo, the internment on Cyprus of illegal immigrants.

1946—August—British open fire on Haifa crowd protesting deportations to Cyprus and kill three people.

1947—January—Truman asks Congress to increase immigration quotas for Jews; Congress stalls.

1947—July 7—Truman urges Congress to act.

1947—July–August—British intercept the *Exodus* with 4,515 DPs aboard; the Jews are later forced to debark in Hamburg, Germany; there are protests from around the world.

1947—August 31—UN Special Committee on Palestine recommends British forces leave the country.

1947—November 29—UN General Assembly authorizes establishment of two states, one Palestinian, the other Jewish.

1948—British launch Operation Deluge in an unsuccessful effort to halt illegal immigration to Palestine.

1948—April 9—The Stern Gang massacres more than two hundred Arabs at Deir Yassin; Arabs retaliate, killing seventy-seven medical personnel.

1948—May 14—Israel declares statehood; five Arab countries declare war on the new nation; the United States and Russia quickly recognize Israel; Great Britain does not.

1948—June 25—Truman signs watered-down immigration bill S.2242 into law despite protests from Jews.

1948—September—UN representative Count Bernadotte negotiates between Israel and the Arabs; he is assassinated by the Stern Gang.

1949—February—A truce is negotiated by UN mediator Ralph Bunche.

1949—December—Israel transfers its capital city from Tel Aviv to Jerusalem over Arab protests.

SOURCE NOTES

Chapter One

1. Yehudit Kleiman and Nina Springer-Aharoni, eds., *The Anguish of Liberation: Testimonies From 1945* (Jerusalem: Yad Vashem, 1995), p. 19.
2. Alan Bullock, *Hitler and Stalin: Parallel Lives* (New York: Alfred A. Knopf, 1992), p. 759.
3. Matt Rosenberg, *"Displaced Jews in Europe: 1945–1951,"* About.com dateline May 19, 1998, Internet: http://geography.about.com/education/geography/library/weekly/aa051898.htm
4. Anita Lasker-Wallfisch, *Inherit the Truth: A Memoir of Survival and the Holocaust* (New York: St. Martin's Press, 2000), p. 97.
5. *Chronicles of the 20th Century* (Mount Kisco, NY: Chronicle Publications, 1987), p. 590.
6. Kleiman and Springer-Aharoni, p. 53.
7. Ibid., p. 58.
8. Ibid., pp. 51–52.
9. Abram L. Sachar, *The Redemption of the Unwanted* (New York: St. Martin's/Marek, 1983), p. 6.
10. Ibid., p. 9.

Chapter Two

1. Academy Award-winning documentary film directed by Mark Jonathan Harris, *The Long Way Home* (First Run Features, 1997).

2. Howard M. Sachar, *A History of the Jews in America* (New York: Alfred A. Knopf, 1992), p. 553.

3. Dwight D. Eisenhower, *Eisenhower's Response to President Truman on Harrison Report,* p. 1. (The Jewish Student Online Research Center—JSOURCE) From *Words of Peace–Words of War,* in *The New York Times,* October 16, 1945. Internet: http://www.us-israel.org^source/holocaust/ike-on-harrison.html

4. Abram L. Sachar, *The Redemption of the Unwanted* (New York: St. Martin's/Marek, 1983), p. 160.

5. Earl G. Harrison, *Report of Earl G. Harrison* (The Jewish Student Online Research Center–JSOURCE) From *Truman's Letter Regarding the Harrison Report on the Treatment of Displaced Jews,* p. 4. Internet: http://www.us-israel.org/jsource/holocaust/dptoc.html

6. *UNRRA and Other Relief Organizations,* courtesy of *Encyclopedia of the Holocaust.* Internet: http://motlc.weisenthal.com/index.html

7. Mark Wyman, *DPs: Europe's Displaced Persons, 1945–1951* (Ithaca, NY: Cornell University Press, 1989), p. 57.

8. Martin Gilbert, *The Boys: The Story of 732 Young Concentration Camp Survivors* (New York: Henry Holt and Company, 1997), p. 262.

9. Yehudit Kleiman and Nina Springer-Aharoni, eds., *The Anguish of Liberation: Testimonies From 1945* (Jerusalem: Yad Vashem, 1995), p. 36.

10. Harrison, p. 5.

11. Ibid., p. 11.

Chapter Three

1. Earl G. Harrison, *Report of Earl G. Harrison* (The Jewish Student Online Research Center—JSOURCE) From *Truman's Letter Regarding the Harrison Report on the Treatment of Displaced Jews,* p. 10. Internet: http://www.us-israel.org^source/holocaust/dptoc.html

2. Howard M. Sachar, *A History of the Jews in America* (New York: Alfred A. Knopf, 1992), p. 555.

3. Ibid.

4. Harrison, p. 5.

5. Ibid.

6. David McCullough, *Truman* (New York: Simon & Schuster, 1992), p. 286.

7. The Jewish Student Online Research Center (JSOURCE), *Truman's Letter Regarding the Harrison Report on the Treatment of Displaced Jews*, pp. 1–2. Internet: http://www.us-israel.org^source/holocaust/dptoc.html

8. Abram L. Sachar, *The Redemption of the Unwanted* (New York: St. Martin's/Marek, 1983), p. 165.

9. Ibid.

10. Ibid., p. 163.

11. *Compton's Interactive Encyclopedia*, 1998.

12. Academy Award-winning documentary film directed by Mark Jonathan Harris, *The Long Way Home* (First Run Features, 1997).

13. Dwight D. Eisenhower, *Eisenhower's Response to President Truman on Harrison Report,* pp. 1–2. (The Jewish Student Online Research Center–JSOURCE) From *Words of Peace–Words of War,* in *The New York Times,* October 16, 1945. Internet: http://www.us-israel.org^source/holocaust/ike-on-harrison.html

14. Ibid., p. 2.

15. Ibid., p. 3.

16. Abram L. Sachar, p. 165.

17. Eisenhower, p. 2.

18. Ted Gottfried, *Eleanor Roosevelt: First Lady of the Twentieth Century* (Danbury, CT: Franklin Watts, 1997), p. 94.

19. Harrison, p. 14.

20. Harris, *The Long Way Home*.

Chapter Four

1. Mark Wyman, *DPs: Europe's Displaced Persons, 1945–1951* (Ithaca, NY: Cornell University Press, 1989), p. 61.

2. Yehudit Kleiman and Nina Springer-Aharoni, eds., *The Anguish of Liberation: Testimonies From 1945* (Jerusalem: Yad Vashem, 1995), p. 61.

3. Aaron Hass, *The Aftermath: Living With the Holocaust* (New York: Cambridge University Press, 1995), p. 186.

4. Ibid., p. 187.

5. Martin Gilbert, *The Boys: The Story of 732 Young Concentration Camp Survivors* (New York: Henry Holt and Company, 1997), p. 265.

6. Wyman, p. 143.

7. Abram L. Sachar, *The Redemption of the Unwanted* (New York: St. Martin's/Marek, 1983), p. 154.

8. Wyman, p. 144.

9. Academy Award-winning documentary film directed by Mark Jonathan Harris, *The Long Way Home* (First Run Features, 1997).

10. Wyman, pp. 144, 170.

11. Ibid., p. 147.

12. Ibid., pp. 147–148.

13. Sachar, p. 156.

14. Ibid., p. 157.

15. Ibid.

16. Ibid., p. 158.

17. Harris, *The Long Way Home*.

Chapter Five

1. *Memo to America: The DP Story; The Final Report of the United States Displaced Persons Commission* (Washington: United States Government Printing Office, 1952), p. 9.

2. *Chronicles of the 20th Century* (Mount Kisco, NY: Chronicle Publications, 1987), p. 279.

3. *Memo to America: The DP Story*, p. 4.

4. Ruth Gruber, *Haven: The Unknown Story of 1,000 World War II Refugees* (New York: Coward-McCann, Inc., 1983), p. 18.

5. Ibid., p. 25.

6. Ibid., pp. 24–25.

7. Howard M. Sachar, *A History of the Jews in America* (New York: Alfred A. Knopf, 1992), p. 493.

8. Gruber, p. 29.

9. Sachar, p. 549.

10. Gruber, p. 71.

11. Ibid., p. 151.

12. Ibid., p. 256.

13. President Harry Truman, *President Truman's Statement and Directive on Displaced Persons,* p. 3 (The Jewish Student Online Research Center—JSOURCE) From *Words of Peace–Words of War,* in *The New York Times,* October 16, 1945. Internet: http://www.us-israel.org^source/holocaust/truman_on_dps.html

14. Matt Rosenberg, *"Displaced Jews in Europe: 1945–1951,"* About.com dateline May 19, 1998, Internet: http://geography.about.com/education/geography/library/weekly/aa051898.htm

15. Sachar, p. 583.

16. Academy Award-winning documentary film directed by Mark Jonathan Harris, *The Long Way Home* (First Run Features, 1997).

17. *Memo to America: The DP Story*, p. 11.

18. Ibid., pp. 10–11.

19. She'erit ha-Pletah, *What Happened to the Jews After the Holocaust?*, Internet: About.com:http//www.holocaust-history.org/...

20. *Memo to America: The DP Story,* p. 11.

21. Ibid., p. 14.

22. Ibid., p. 15.

23. Ibid., p. 14.

24. Ibid., p. 17.

25. Ibid., pp. 26–27.

26. She'erit ha-Pletah, *What Happened to the Jews.*

27. Emma Lazarus, *The New Colossus: Inscription for the Statue of Liberty, New York Harbor,* in *Bartlett's Familiar Quotations: Fourteenth Edition* (Boston: Little, Brown and Company, 1968), p. 817.

Chapter Six

1. Mark Wyman, *DPs: Europe's Displaced Persons, 1945–1951* (Ithaca, NY: Cornell University Press, 1989), p. 169.

2. Ibid., p. 173.

3. Eleanor H. Ayer, *The Survivors* (San Diego: Lucent Books, 1998), p. 27.

4. Wyman, p. 175.

5. Ibid., p. 174.

6. Abram L. Sachar, *The Redemption of the Unwanted* (New York: St. Martin's/Marek, 1983), p. 42.

7. Ibid., p. 166.

8. Wyman, p. 86.

9. I. F. Stone, *Underground to Palestine and Reflections Thirty Years Later* (New York: Pantheon Books, 1978), p. 25.

10. She'erit ha-Pletah, Internet: about.com:http//www.holocaust-history.org/...

11. Koppel S. Pinson, *Jewish Life in Liberated Germany—A Study of the Jewish DPs* in *Jewish Social Studies* 9 (April 1947), p. 117.

12. Wyman, p. 138.

13. Sachar, p. 167.

14. She'erit ha-Pletah, Internet.

15. Michael Berenbaum, *The World Must Know* (Boston: Little, Brown, and Company, 1993), p. 208.

16. Aaron Hass, *The Aftermath: Living With the Holocaust* (New York: Cambridge University Press, 1995), p. 98.

17. Sachar, p. 166.

18. Academy Award-winning documentary film directed by Mark Jonathan Harris, *The Long Way Home* (First Run Features, 1997).

Chapter Seven

1. I. F. Stone, *Underground to Palestine and Reflections Thirty Years Later* (New York: Pantheon Books, 1978), pp. 223–224.
2. Abram L. Sachar, *The Redemption of the Unwanted* (New York: St. Martin's/Marek, 1983), p. 182.
3. *Chronicles of the 20th Century* (Mount Kisco, NY: Chronicle Publications, 1987), p. 601.
4. Ibid., p. 613.
5. Sachar, p. 183.
6. *Chronicles*, p. 614.
7. William H. Honan, *Rudolph Patzert, 88; Transported Jews to Palestine After War*, Obituary in *The New York Times,* February 21, 2000, p. A 17.
8. Yoram Kaniuk, Trans. *Seymour Simckes: Commander of the Exodus* (New York: Grove Press, 2000), p. 143.
9. Ibid., p. 144.
10. Ibid., p. 140.
11. Ibid., p. 155.
12. Sachar, pp. 186–187.

Chapter Eight

1. *Compton's Interactive Encyclopedia*, 1998.
2. *Chronicles of the 20th Century* (Mount Kisco, NY: Chronicle Publications, 1987), p. 632.
3. Howard M. Sachar, *A History of the Jews in America* (New York: Alfred A. Knopf, 1992), p. 560.
4. Mark Wyman, *DPs: Europe's Displaced Persons, 1945–1951* (Ithaca, NY: Cornell University Press, 1989), p. 155.

5. Abram L. Sachar, *The Redemption of the Unwanted* (New York: St. Martin's/Marek, 1983), p. 242.
6. Howard M. Sachar, p. 602.
7. Abram L. Sachar, p. 245.
8. Ibid., p. 247.
9. Ibid., p. 258.
10. *Chronicles,* p. 642.
11. Ibid.
12. Wyman, p. 155.
13. *Chronicles,* p. 651.
14. Ibid., p. 652.
15. Ibid., p. 671.
16. W. H. Auden, *Selected Poems* (New York: Vintage International, 1989), p. 86.
17. Malcolm J. Proudfoot, *European Refugees: 1939–1952: A Study in Forced Population Movement* (Evanston, IL: Northwestern University Press, 1956), pp. 359–360. Quoted by Matt Rosenberg, *Displaced Jews in Europe: Charts and Bibliography,* p. 3. Internet: http://geography.about.com/library/weekly/aa051898b.htm?pid=2820&cob=home
18. Ibid.

GLOSSARY

anti-Semitism—irrational hatred and persecution of Jews

Bricha (flight)—Zionist program that organized an exodus of Jews from Eastern Europe

concentration camp—place of confinement for anti-Nazis and Jews; workplace; slaughterhouse

crematorium—ovens disposing of the bodies of those gassed in the death camps

death camps—concentration camps equipped for mass killing

displaced person (DP)—one driven from his or her home by war

DP camp—holding area for victims of war; often former Nazi concentration camps

Final Solution—the Nazi plan to kill off the entire Jewish population of Europe

fraternization—relationships between American soldiers and German civilians

genocide—the killing of a whole race, people, or nation

ghetto—originally a sealed-off area where Jews were forced to live

Haganah—the underground Jewish army, which fought the British in Palestine; later the official Israeli army, which fought the Arabs in the 1948–1949 invasion

Harrison Report—findings of inspection of DP camps by Earl G. Harrison for President Truman

Holocaust—systematic extermination of six million European Jews by the Nazis internment camps—British holding areas for illegal immigrants

International Relief Organization (IRO)—group that replaced UNRRA to run DP camps

Israel—the Jewish state; formerly Palestine

Jewish Brigade—Palestinian Jews who fought alongside the British in World War II

Kielce—city where postwar massacre of Jews by Poles took place

Operation Igloo—the imprisonment of illegal Jewish immigrants on the island of Cyprus

Palestine—the country that would become Israel; homeland claimed by Zionists for Jews

pogrom—organized massacre of Jews in Czarist Russia

S.2242—the Senate bill to increase immigration quotas and signed by President Truman despite "many defects"

shlichim—individual Zionists who acted as guides for Jews fleeing Eastern Europe

stateless—having no homeland to which one can return

The Joint—nickname for the American Joint Distribution Committee, which helped postwar Jewish refugees

The Protocols of the Learned Elders of Zion—1897 document forged by Russian secret police to foment pogroms against Jews

United Nations Relief and Rehabilitation Agency (UNRRA)—UN organization dealing with refugees

Zionist—one who favors the establishment of a Jewish nation

FOR MORE INFORMATION

Ayer, Eleanor H. *The Survivors*. San Diego: Lucent Books, 1998.

Browning, Christopher R. *Ordinary Men: Reserve Police Battalion 101 and the Final Solution in Poland*. New York: HarperCollins Publishers, 1992.

Fogelman, Eva. *Conscience & Courage: Rescuers of Jews During the Holocaust*. New York: Anchor Books/Doubleday, 1994.

Gilbert, Martin. *The Boys: Triumph Over Adversity*. London: Weidenfeld & Nicolson, 1996.

Gruber, Ruth. *Haven: The Unknown Story of 1,000 World War II Refugees*. New York: Coward-McCann, Inc., 1983.

Hass, Aaron. *The Aftermath*. Cambridge: Cambridge University Press, 1995.

McCollough, David. *Truman*. New York: Simon & Schuster, 1992.

Morris, Benny. *Righteous Victims: A History of the Zionist-Arab Conflict, 1881–1999*. New York: Alfred A. Knopf, 1999.

Rosenberg, Maxine B. *Hiding to Survive: Stories of Jewish Children Rescued from the Holocaust*. New York: Clarion Books, 1994.

Sachar, Abram L. *The Redemption of the Unwanted.* New York: St. Martin's/Marek, 1983.

Shirer, William L. *The Rise and Fall of the Third Reich: A History of Nazi Germany.* New York: Simon & Schuster, 1960.

Spiegelman, Art. *Maus: A Survivor's Tale: My Father Bleeds History.* New York: Pantheon Books [paper], 1986.

———. *Maus II: A Survivor's Tale: And Here My Troubles Begin.* New York: Pantheon Books, 1991.

Wyman, Mark. *DPs: Europe's Displaced Persons, 1945–1951.* Ithaca: Cornell University Press [Paperback], 1998.

Yoran, Shalom. *The Defiant: A True Story.* New York: St. Martin's Press, 1996.

Recommended Films

Schindler's List, directed by Steven Spielberg, 1993.

Shoah (French documentary), directed by Claude Lanzmann, 1985.

The Long Way Home (documentary), directed by Mark Jonathan Harris, 1997.

Internet Sites

(All have links to related sites.)

The United States Holocaust Memorial Museum
  www.ushmm.org/

The Holocaust: An Historical Summary
  www.ushmm.org/education/history.html

Holocaust Resources on the World Wide Web
www.fred.net/nhhs/html/hololink.htm

The Jewish Student Online Research Center (JSOURCE)
www.us-israel.org/jsource

Remembering the Holocaust
yarra.vicnet.net.au/~aragorn/holocaus.htm

Matt Rosenberg, "Displaced Jews in Europe: 1945–1951"
geography.about.com/education/geography/library/weekly/aa051898.htm

She'erit ha-Pletah
about.com:http//www.holocaust-history.org/...

INDEX

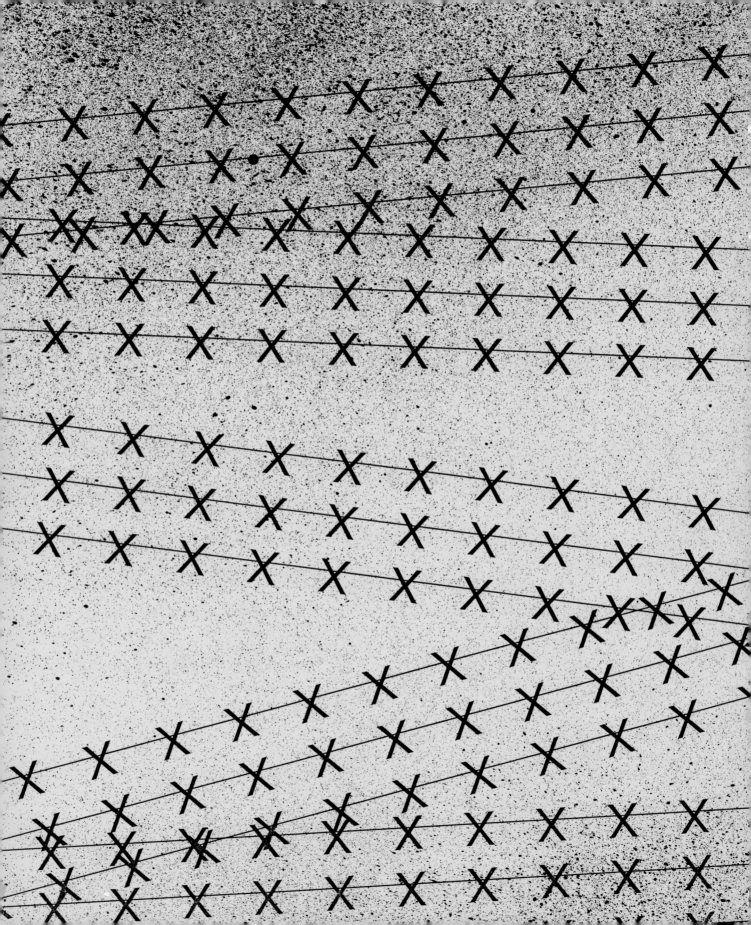